M000297461

THE LEADERSHIP
CONTINUUM

THE LEADERSHIP CONTINUUM

How Flexing across the Seven Facets of
Leadership Increases Effectiveness

by
Bill Heiden, Theresa Hoffman, and
Cathleen Swody, PhD

Thrive Leadership Press

© 2020 by Bill Heiden, Theresa Hoffman, and Cathleen Swody

All rights reserved. This book or any portion thereof may not be reproduced or used in any manner whatsoever without the express written permission of the publisher except for the use of brief quotations in a book review.

ISBN: 978-0-578-76142-8 (paperback)

I would like to dedicate this book to my wife and life partner, Cristina. I met Cristina while on assignment in Italy many years ago and she agreed to join me on our life's adventures. She has always been there for me with a warm embrace or a kick in the pants (depending on what I required), a fresh pasta dish, and a glass of wine! *Ti voglio bene cara.*
—Bill

To my husband, John—thanks for your unwavering support through thick and thin.
—Theresa

To Steve with love and gratitude.
—Cathleen

CONTENTS

PREFACE

I have been a CEO at both private and publicly traded companies for the last fifteen years and have been leading teams in the health care industry for more than thirty years. I have experienced the joys (and challenges) of leading successful teams in the United States and abroad—living and working overseas for several years and dealing with all the special challenges that come with those assignments (e.g., foreign languages and different cultural norms). I am passionate about effective leadership, having seen the tremendous influence that leaders can have on organizations. I have also seen and coached aspiring leaders who needed to improve their leadership effectiveness. As I have thought about the tools that effective leaders employ, I have begun to appreciate that the best leaders modify their approach based on the facts of the situation. The very best, most effective leaders have acquired an ability to vary their approach across key leadership skills. Understanding these seven leadership attributes—and how and when one can and should flex across them—is the first step to enhancing leadership effectiveness. Leaders need to learn to be comfortable with a heterogeneity of leadership styles depending upon the specifics of the situation. Gaining an awareness of one's natural tendencies is the next step. These natural leadership approaches can be considered natural strengths—but they can be a weakness if the leader doesn't acquire the ability to employ alternate approaches when necessary. Finally, attaining an enhanced ability to flex across these facets of leadership will increase a leader's ultimate effectiveness. This book, *The Leadership Continuum: How Flexing across the Seven Facets of Leadership Increases Effectiveness*, will help aspiring leaders grow and develop and help experienced leaders become even more effective.

I wrote this book with two fellow leadership experts who share my passion for the power of great leadership. Theresa Hoffman and Dr. Cathleen Swody are the founders of Thrive Leadership, a firm that partners with organizations across industries to develop the leadership talent needed to get sustainable business results.

Theresa Hoffman has worked with hundreds of senior leaders over the years. Her coaching approach gives leaders a deep understanding of their unique strengths, weaknesses, and tendencies. Once aware of these, leaders can manage themselves to have the greatest positive effect on other people, their teams, and their organizations. Based on her extensive experience, Theresa shares practical insights and exercises in this book that she has seen successfully used to hone and strengthen various leadership skills.

Dr. Cathleen Swody is an industrial/organizational psychologist whose driving force is applying research insights to help leaders reach their goals. For over fifteen years, she has debriefed countless assessments of leaders and potential leaders and has studied what distinguishes excellent leaders from the rest. To share her passion for the topic, Cathleen has served on the University of Connecticut faculty, where she taught leadership to MBA students. Based on this expertise, Cathleen connected the book's insights to research.

CHAPTER 1

INTRODUCTION

E mily, a high-potential young manager, came to see me early one evening when we were both in the office working. I always make time to mentor up-and-coming leaders, so I put the report I was reading down and asked Emily to have a seat. Having come up through the commercial organization, she led a small but high-performing team of five, and we were grooming Emily for bigger, broader responsibilities in the future. I had a strong conviction that she was a talented young manager who had significant leadership potential.

Emily explained that she had been reading some articles on leadership and was particularly focused on some famous leaders being strong and rapid decision makers. She explained that she was, by nature, a bit more of a deep thinker who liked to consider all angles of a decision before jumping in. Did I think that her natural tendency was going to limit her growth and prospects as a leader? But she was also prepared to challenge what she had read. "Shouldn't all great leaders," Emily asked, "take the time to consider the consequences of their decisions?"

That conversation with Emily got me thinking. Although it is true that great leaders do have the ability to make decisions quickly and decisively when necessary, it does not mean that they don't also have the ability to wait and be more reflective in certain situations. In fact, really talented leaders can flex, depending on the situation, across a continuum of decision-making agility. It is also true that most leaders, both experienced and less experienced like Emily, have a natural tendency toward one side of the continuum or the other. But effective leaders are the ones who learn how to move across the continuum and to deploy the appropriate skills depending on the particulars of the situation and the people involved.

When I have brought up the need to learn and adopt different styles for different situations, a few young leaders have responded, "Well, that's my leadership style, and the team I lead will have to adapt to it." I remind them that leadership is measured by effectiveness. Although some teams might accept the "wrong" leadership style for a given situation, there is also a good chance that they won't respond well to it—or more subtly, the leader is less effective than they could have been if they'd employed a more appropriate style. For example, a leader's poorly thought-through decision might appear to be accepted by the team, but the team's follow-through will likely be weak and characterized by low energy.

As my coauthors and I thought about the concept of a leadership continuum on decision-making, we found that there were several other key leadership facets that had a similar yet seemingly opposite set of underlying skills that great leaders appear to balance. But like decision-making, as discussed earlier, we found that each end of a facet's continuum had its time and place for use. We initially came up with a long list of leadership topics, but we worked hard to consolidate it down to seven key leadership facets to explore along the leadership continuum.

My conversation with Emily that evening really got me thinking. It was the stimulus for us to conclude that we could help current and aspiring leaders see the benefits of understanding the leadership facets' continuum. Perhaps we could help people identify their natural tendencies (which can be natural strengths...or natural weaknesses), raise their awareness of and sensitivity to the tendencies of others (employees, colleagues, and bosses), and develop the skill to understand when and how to flex across the continuum for maximum effectiveness. That is our premise behind—and the aspiration for—writing this book.

CHAPTER 2

EFFECTIVE LEADERSHIP

We have been practicing, studying, coaching, and teaching leadership for decades. We've seen firsthand how leaders can learn, grow, and evolve; identify areas for professional development; and, through great effort, become the influential leaders they aspire to be. We have also seen examples of leaders who don't develop, and their effectiveness and professional growth remain limited. We have also seen the amazing things that great leaders can achieve in organizations—how they create lofty visions for what divisions or companies can become and can achieve, how creative and aspirational plans are developed that map out a blueprint for how to get there, and how excellent communication and leadership can result in strong execution and the achievement—or surpassing—of those lofty visions.

We believe that there are several different types of great leaders, and this book, unlike many others, does not lay out a few must-have leadership characteristics. Rather, we believe that there are certain leadership traits that really great leaders should have the ability to flex across and that no one leadership style fits well for every situation. Instead, it can employ a continuum of styles across those characteristics that enables maximum leadership effectiveness.

This is not to say that there is not a solid list of things that nearly all great leaders do effectively. For example, nearly all great leaders are effective communicators and have the ability to convey information in a clear, concise, and compelling fashion. Some are inspirational orators with large groups, and some are better one-on-one, but you would be hard-pressed to find a truly great leader who was not an effective communicator. But sometimes a leader should be more of a listener than a talker. We will speak more about that in a few minutes.

A leader's ability to communicate effectively is often directed to inspire and drive individuals and teams to exert significant effort toward achieving a set of goals. In leadership parlance, inspiring high employee engagement means that leaders can drive employees and teams to exert significant discretionary effort. Great team achievements have almost always been associated with high engagement and significant discretionary effort. This significant effort and drive to achieve or exceed goals directly result from the leader's effective communication.

Another related concept used to describe great leaders is that of inspiring followership. When a leader says, "Let's tackle that summit over yonder," and then marches off purposefully in that direction, what happens if no one follows? Great leaders have a formula for engendering followership that employs various leadership skills (including the good communication mentioned earlier). When they set a course, individuals, teams, divisions, and whole companies follow happily. Successful leaders use a variety of tools to flex across the continuum of key leadership facets in such a way that people do what the leader needs them to do…because they want to do it.

Ultimately, a leader's effectiveness is measured in results, and great leaders achieve great results. At the most basic level, results are achievements against a set of goals. Measurable goals (with numbers) are best for assessing leadership effectiveness, although we acknowledge that not all goals are quantifiable. Good examples of quantitative goals are annual revenue targets, shareholder return metrics, or manufacturing productivity measures. You will find that many seemingly qualitative goals can indeed be measured quantitively. For example, things like employee satisfaction can be measured with scored questionnaires.

The true test of effective leadership comes over time. For example, good judgment, an important skill of great leaders, can only be truly tested over time. One good decision is a great start, but a demonstration of strong judgment over time (which does not need to be 100 percent or perfect) is the true test of a successful leader. Does a leader create followership that has durability over time, through both successful *and* challenging times? Does the leader inspire sustainable long-term effort and high performance? Again, we're not talking about a requisite of perfect performance over time but rather that the true measure of a leader's effectiveness can best be measured over time.

In summary, this book does not endeavor to cover a discrete set of must-have leadership skills but rather to encourage leaders to think about the seven key leadership facets, understand and appreciate that there are benefits to being able to flex across the continuum of those facets, identify their personal bias (toward one or the other side of the continuum), and then learn when and how to flex across the continuum. Effective leaders are lifelong learners. You can be a great leader and still have room to learn to be even better. We believe that this book can help the new or aspiring leader and the most experienced leader.

As the world around us changes, leaders must continue to evolve to achieve maximum effectiveness. The generations of people we lead change (baby boomers to millennials), as do the challenges we face over time (working remotely through a pandemic); thus our approach may need to change. We should all strive to stretch those leadership skills to get better and be even more effective tomorrow than yesterday.

We encourage all leaders to develop across the full continuum of leadership facets. In this book, we give examples of where and how one or the other side of that facet's continuum might be worth employing. To take a simple example, if the building is on fire, decisive action is clearly required. However, if you are considering taking the company in a new strategic direction that involves significant implications, a more thoughtful and structured approach to the decision would be advisable. The same great leader is presented with two different choices and should be employing two different decision-making styles based on the situations. For the naturally decisive leader, the fire emergency response comes easily, but perhaps the path to managing the decision for a new corporate strategy is not so straightforward.

Conversely, while a more thoughtful leader would perhaps have an easier time managing the change in corporate strategy, they might also be the one who hesitates in calling out a plan to exit the building on fire quickly. We believe that the first step is a conscious understanding of which situations call for which approach, followed by practical pointers on implementing the approach. Over time, and with practice, leaders can learn to instinctively evaluate and move to that spot on the continuum to maximize their leadership effectiveness.

This book is useful for even the most experienced and effective leaders looking to tune up in a couple of areas, it is valuable for newer leaders who are still learning as they go and desiring some additional leadership food for thought, and it is an excellent starting point for aspiring young leaders to begin their development on a path to become our next generation of great leaders.

CHAPTER 3

THE LEADERSHIP CONTINUUM ACROSS SEVEN KEY LEADERSHIP FACETS

M any books describe a list of must-have key leadership characteristics. Some books focus on one key characteristic— for example, Angela Duckworth's best-selling book *Grit: The Power of Passion and Perseverance* (2016).

This book takes a different approach by focusing on a short list of key leadership facets. The flexibility and agility to move across these seven skills can maximize effectiveness. We started with a much longer list of leadership skills, but we worked hard to narrow it down by consolidating some leadership skills into one broader term and eliminating others. We wanted to avoid redundancy and focus our work on the most important facets of leadership, where the ability to flex across a continuum was vital.

Throughout the book, we will refer to the two extremes of each continuum simply for clarity. Importantly, we refer to a continuum for each facet of leadership because the best strategy is sometimes somewhere in the middle of the two extremes. In chapter 11, we'll cover the times when an in-between response is best. Equally important, sometimes a leader will choose to start at one end of the continuum and then move toward the other end as the conversation progresses. The very title of this book captures the fundamental concept that leaders must have the ability to flex and move across the continuum of the seven facets of leadership.

Our final list of the seven key facets of leadership is as follows:

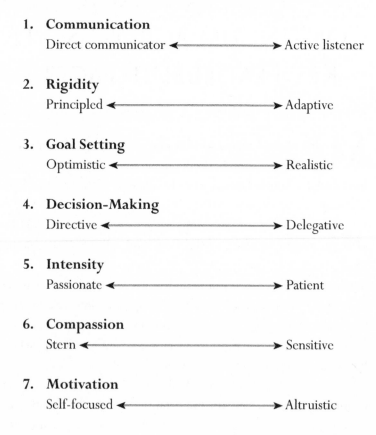

1. **Communication**

   Direct communicator ◄─────────► Active listener

2. **Rigidity**

   Principled ◄─────────► Adaptive

3. **Goal Setting**

   Optimistic ◄─────────► Realistic

4. **Decision-Making**

   Directive ◄─────────► Delegative

5. **Intensity**

   Passionate ◄─────────► Patient

6. **Compassion**

   Stern ◄─────────► Sensitive

7. **Motivation**

   Self-focused ◄─────────► Altruistic

CHAPTER 4

FACET 1: COMMUNICATION

Direct communicator ◄————————► Active listener

G reat leaders are great communicators. Many times, when we say that someone is a great communicator, people immediately think of the inspiring speaker in front of a large group. But before you conclude that that isn't you, let me explain what we mean by *communicator*. First, communicating can occur orally or in writing, and it can take place one-on-one, in a small group, or on a stage in front of five hundred people. Although presenting effectively to a large group is one form of communication, few people have that particular gift—and you will find that most people who do have to work for many years to perfect it. In other words, there are plenty of great leaders who are not comfortable on the big stage but who are wonderfully effective communicators in small groups and one-on-one. Because the smaller group and one-on-one settings are the most common and frequent forums for communication, we'll focus our discussion on maximizing effectiveness in these areas. Effective communication is a critical skill set for all great leaders.

When we talk about a communicator's effectiveness, we refer to the person's ability to communicate their message compellingly and clearly or whether the communicator effectively motivates people to do something. Many books have been written on effective communication and the science and art behind it.

Where we want to make a distinction on this facet is by ensuring that leaders have or develop an ability to communicate the outbound message directly and to move to the other side of the continuum and have the ability to just listen. There are plenty of opportunities for leaders to speak, but, more importantly, there are times when they should simply sit and actively listen, times when they should wait for others to contribute, and times when their role is to actively draw others in to communicate.

For example, many effective leaders regularly employ the what-do-you-think-we-should-do question when someone asks them for direction to solve a problem. I recently had a young manager come to me for advice on a problem that he had run into. Jim was relatively new to managing a team, so I welcomed the opportunity to sit down for a discussion. It was not as significant a conversation as I'd had with Emily (from a leadership strategy perspective), and the issue we discussed was actually no longer a problem for the team. Still, Jim wanted to confirm whether he had handled it well. When I asked him how he had approached the problem, he took me through what had happened, how he had been thinking through how best to respond, and how the situation eventually worked itself out naturally. It was a great opportunity to have a conversation with this young manager about one of the key strategies for leading: the do-nothing-right-away strategy. Often, a situation does not call for action, and in fact, a rapid intervention can make the ultimate outcome worse than it otherwise would have been. The do-nothing response typically goes hand in hand with the monitor-closely approach, with an intervention ready if the situation calls for it.

As our discussion continued, it was clear that there was a future intervention opportunity if things did not naturally continue in the positive direction that we both hoped for. It was also apparent that there were some real benefits to the organization for allowing this situation to run its natural course. I became convinced that the outcome of immediate intervention by this young manager or myself would have likely yielded a worse outcome for the organization. My conversation with Jim focused on helping this new leader see the benefits of sometimes stepping

> ### More on Jim and "Stepping Back"
>
> *It's natural for a new manager to tend toward immediate, aggressive overmanagement initially or, alternatively, a more tentative wait-to-intervene style. A good mentor will stay close to a new manager to provide coaching on when to zoom out...or zoom in. Naturally, action-oriented managers like Jim may be somewhat uncomfortable initially not intervening in some situations. Jim's specific case provided his manager with a nice opportunity to reinforce that Jim had pursued the right approach (to a low-risk/cost decision for his team) and to remind Jim that if he did want to do something, it would most productively be doing some contingency planning in the (low likelihood) event that plan A did not play out as forecasted.*

back to let things unfold naturally. We also discussed how he could now use this window of time to do some contingency planning to be ready if things did not progress as expected.

Another situation that top leaders often encounter is when two people or groups have challenges communicating effectively. Although a direct intervention by the leader may be necessary, the leader should often choose not to intervene and instead direct the two individuals or groups to meet and sort it out themselves (perhaps with some wise words from the leader on how to do that effectively).

Sometimes it is best for top leaders to just sit quietly and observe. Leaders who lead other leaders will often find themselves in large forums where some people assume that the most senior leader has to take the reins. But experienced leaders will often use the opportunity for observation—to watch how the next-level leaders enable future feedback on effectiveness or see how others in the group contribute, which can inform the identification and developmental needs of talent across the organization. I have been in many meetings where I was the most senior person in the room, and someone asked if I'd like to open the meeting or provide some introductory comments. When I've offered any commentary at the outset of a meeting, the group looked to me throughout the meeting to lead. Whereas if I initially responded, "No, I'm good. Carry on," I established a very different environment in which I was not the leader. That simple opening statement (or lack thereof) worked every time to clearly establish that I was a nonleading participant for the meeting duration.

I have tried hard throughout my career to be a good active listener. As some wise person once said, "You don't learn anything when you're talking." I listen actively to try to learn new things from my colleagues; most are experts in their fields, and they help make me a better executive and enable better decision-making. I also have many years of experience that have proven to me that decision-making and problem-solving are better served by active listening and questioning. Active listening is another way of saying "pay attention." Listen to what the speaker is saying, listen to the tone and the emotion behind how they are saying it, and listen for what is not being said. Can additional facts be requested that would make or break the case for what is being presented? Is there a certain emotion that is being communicated that might be worth exploring further?

I remember hearing an acquisition proposal from an executive in our business development group for which the facts presented were not terribly compelling, but the executive appeared incredibly enthusiastic about the opportunity. While several people zeroed in on the less-than-compelling facts of the proposal and the chances of moving forward continued to decline, one active listener asked the executive, "Evan, you seem particularly excited about this project. What am I missing?" It turned out that Evan had a tangential—but interesting—set of data that challenged the standard approach we had used to evaluate the opportunity. Once we got him talking about that, it was clear that we needed to gather some additional information before making any decisions on this opportunity. The group left the meeting excited to collect additional information for their proposal. While this particular acquisition ultimately did not move forward, the team clearly felt that we had really listened, and they were energized to move on to the next opportunity.

An important project had just started at one company where I was working, and although there were many people engaged and working hard on it, it seemed that parts of the project were not integrated into the whole. We had two talented young leaders who were heading the effort, but I was concerned. This was a perfect time for a leader to employ active and effective communication. I took the opportunity to organize a broad group kickoff meeting, during which I actively communicated my enthusiasm and support for the team and their leaders. We then listed the areas where we needed to ensure that we had coordinated action plans, timelines, and budgets. The team worked to pull those items together within the agreed-upon time frame, essentially creating their own road map for managing this complex project as a team.

Sometimes a leader observes a discussion getting stuck. Perhaps the group is not really clear on the objective, or perhaps someone has inserted a conversation killer into the discussion ("Pursuing that particular strategy would be doomed from the start"). Those are great times for a leader to step in and get the conversation back on a constructive, focused path: "Those are all interesting points. Now let's refocus on the goal of this meeting, which is…"

As you can see, there are times when leaders should clearly use a more direct style of communication. Still, there are also opportunities for leaders to step back and actively listening to achieve maximum effectiveness. Deciding when to use which mode of communication is key. The following is a list of cues that leaders can anchor to when thinking about where on the communication continuum they should gravitate to maximize effectiveness. Perhaps it's obvious, but it's perfectly normal to move across the continuum by employing different approaches in one meeting or encounter. You might start as a very direct communicator to diffuse a difficult situation between two managers only to gravitate to a more active listener as the two people begin to interact and sort things out themselves directly. When considering the appropriate communication style, think about the following:

Direct communicator ←⎯⎯⎯→ Active listener

Consider when	*Consider when*
You are the obvious expert	Someone else is the expert
Diffusing a tense situation	Letting others sort things out
Framing a conversation	Engendering outcome ownership
Focusing a conversation	Observing and allowing others to lead

Chapter 5

Facet 2: Rigidity

Principled ◄———————————————► Adaptive

There's a great line attributed to Alexander Hamilton: "If you don't stand for something, you'll fall for anything." Simply put, it's important for individuals—and even more critical for successful leaders—to have a core set of beliefs that guide their decision-making and establish clear direction in their lives. Most leaders would agree that they would not endorse doing anything illegal to achieve a desirable business objective. Presumably, the basis for that response is a core belief in respecting the law. Most successful leaders establish early in their lives, or develop over time and with experience, a core set of beliefs and principles that guide their behavior and decision-making. Some simple examples that you likely heard early in your life include "Treat others the way you would like to be treated" and "If you don't have anything nice to say, don't say anything at all." Most leaders develop an even longer list of strong principles and beliefs that greatly influence their decision-making and approach to leading.

The writer Ayn Rand's philosophical approach, known as objectivism, describes how a clear set of core beliefs is essential for dealing with highly complex problems. Only by evaluating these complex issues against a core set of principles can one establish an objective response. For example, on the political front, it's easy to be swayed by the emotional rhetoric from either side of a complex issue, when a better approach is almost always to step back and objectively view the facts against a set of principles. Although individuals with strong core principles may be able to more easily clear through the rhetoric to make a principled assessment as to which approach is best, those very principles can sometimes get in the way of a good outcome in the leadership setting, as we will explain.

Here again, the best leaders can flex across this rigidity continuum. There are times when leaders must stay inflexible and true to strongly held principles while other times call for more openness to core beliefs being challenged or acknowledging and respecting the different beliefs of another.

Firmly held and important principles are those that successful leaders never (or rarely) stray from; nor do they allow their organizations to behave in a manner inconsistent with those principles. For example, suppose the leader and company have a firm zero tolerance position for deviations from a certain policy. In that case, an employee's termination knowingly moving away from that policy is a straightforward decision.

Having a core set of principles is also valuable when confronted with uncertainty and challenges that simply have no right answer. Should we pay that disgruntled departing employee their bonus even though it is not explicitly defined in our policy? It might be less costly to pay the departing employee versus the costs of a dragged-out legal battle. One company might have a strong principled position on this issue that results in one decision. In contrast, another company might approach this question in a more open manner, depending on the facts of the situation.

A strong set of core principles also guides the leader and their organization to act consistently across similar types of uncertainties, which can help in the long run. People (both inside and outside the organization) get a strong sense of what they can expect. Outside the company, you might hear, "That's a company/leader who never backs down in cases like this, so we better just drop it." Internally, a strong set of principles from top leadership and the company enable decisiveness throughout the organization as decision makers understand some of the basic frameworks for key decisions. For example, I have always encouraged business risk-taking and small pilots in organizations that I've overseen. I talk openly about that principle and try to support it with positive reinforcement: celebrating low-cost failures and highlighting successes that started with an unproven pilot. My goal is for people throughout the organization to understand that we want them to try out new ideas and then tell us about both the successes—so that we can expand on them—and the failures—so that we can all learn from them.

The most successful leaders also train themselves to be open, to be challenged on the principles and structure of approach. I've had long-held beliefs that have been successfully challenged because I remained open to listening and learning. This is especially important for more seasoned leaders. They run the risk of becoming too rigid and not allowing long-held beliefs to be questioned by younger or less experienced people with different beliefs and

Celebrating Failure?

You may be wondering, how the heck do you celebrate failure without appearing to be encouraging it? This aspect of leadership does require some "finesse." One critical element for leaders encouraging risk-taking is to ensure that teams are thinking through the "cost" of failure. The cost may simply be the expense of the unsuccessful program. But sometimes the potential cost is broader; for example, failure might cause reputational damage to the company. A part of the leader's job in encouraging risk is to communicate and reinforce (for example, through Q&A) the thought process that needs to go into that risk-taking. Then, when (and if) the risk does not work out, the "celebration" needs to include explicitly reinforcing how a team assessed the downside risk (low) and then key learnings from the project—perhaps learnings that will better inform another decision / project.

experiences. Long-tenured leaders' experience sets can become outdated and may simply develop into an incorrect frame to use against current issues. My own experience has taught me to be open to the reality that my data set and experiences may become dated over time—more so as every year goes by. Some of my basic assumptions may be wrong. I try to view these as opportunities to learn, usually by requesting more data to confirm and then correct or update my assumption set. It also allows me to delegate the construct of some company approaches or principles in specific areas where I learn over time that someone else has a more current and appropriate level of experience and judgment. For example, pricing decisions can present a complex set of challenges in health care, and although I was intimately involved in these decisions earlier in my career, I learned to delegate some aspects of pricing strategies to others in the organization who have similar core principles to mine but who have more current and relevant experience.

I have witnessed significant change in the complex area of health care pricing over the last ten years. It is especially in these times of fundamental change and complexity that leaders must be open to having their basic principles and assumptions challenged or risk making poor decisions based on an outdated set of principles. Leaders are most vulnerable to poor decisions (and job loss) based on outdated frameworks resulting from significant industry change. Blockbuster Video made a major strategic investment decision by making customer DVD movie pickup easier by moving from stand-alone stores to even easier pickup at local grocery store kiosks, but they missed the more significant threat of online movie availability. Someone had a basic principle or assumption about the importance of improving DVD movie pickup efficiency that turned out to be outdated and ultimately fatal.

Perhaps it is obvious, but the most successful leaders tend toward the left on the rigidity continuum, naturally basing their leadership and decisions on a strong set of core principles. But these same successful leaders have the ability and willingness to lean right on this continuum, being open to challenging their own key principles in times of significant change.

It is interesting to note that one of the fundamental reasons that great leaders can be open to having their basic assumptions challenged is that they have an even more fundamental set of principles on which to fall back. I am reminded of a meeting during which my head of human resources challenged one of our company's long-standing basic personnel policies with a new policy proposal. I believe one of the reasons that I was able to step back and objectively evaluate the new proposal (challenging my long-held belief that the original policy was appropriate and should not be changed) was that I could assess the new concept against an even more fundamental core set of principles on how I believe a company should treat its employees.

When should you stick to your guns on basic principles, and when should you take a more adaptive leadership approach? The following is a list of scenarios when leaders should consider one or the other approach in terms of rigidity:

Principled ←———————————→ Adaptive

Consider when	*Consider when*
Relying on core beliefs to make decisions	Being receptive to having your core beliefs challenged
Applying strong principles to your leadership approach	Acknowledging and respecting the different beliefs of others
Staying true to your deeply held beliefs	Remaining open to listening to and learning from others
Expecting the company to act consistently with your core beliefs	Taking a depends-on-the-facts-of-the-situation approach
Taking a strong principled position on an issue	Requesting data to correct or update your assumptions
Acting consistently across similar types of uncertainties	Delegating decisions to those with more current or relevant experience

Chapter 6

Facet 3: Goal Setting

Optimistic ◄─────────────► Realistic

The science and art of planning and goal setting for leaders is a fascinating area of discussion. Great leaders balance the seemingly schizophrenic two-headed monster of unbridled optimism and unlimited potential with a need for practicality and realism.

There are many stories of great leaders setting ambitious goals that inspired amazing achievements. John Kennedy set a goal to be the first country to put a man on the moon at exactly the point in time when we did not have the technology—and when all we knew was that our rival in that race (the Soviet Union) did. In business, from Walt Disney (of Disney film and entertainment fame) to Steve Jobs (Apple) to Elon Musk (Tesla), these leaders set lofty change-the-world goals that inspired employees, investors, and the general public. Great leaders who have durability don't have just a singular vision; they tend to build on and add overtime to that initial vision. Observe how Apple first inspired us to reimagine the computer (Mac), how to listen to music (iPod), how to connect and interact digitally with the world (iPhone), and how to put that same capability on our wrist (Apple Watch). People sometimes have the misconception that all extraordinary leaders have one grand vision when, in fact, most leaders are consistently recreating and updating their visions, thus reinspiring their organizations over time.

Creating optimistic goals for an organization or group can be a tough skill for practical young leaders to embrace. It's Monday, and although you may feel that your organization needs a lift—something big and inspiring to reenergize things—it is a daunting challenge to ask yourself to inspire and convey a vision. For most people, creating a vision and inspiration for an organization can be even more effective when a group of leaders creates it. For example, if a leader senses the need for vision for their organization, one useful path forward can be to bring together a group of trusted lieutenants to cocreate a vision for the future.

I remember going through this exercise as a young leader when I took over an underperforming team. At an off-site meeting, I began by asking the attendees if they thought they were the best team in our division. They did. Then I took them through our performance numbers, where we could all see that the data showed that our performance ranked dead last compared to all our peers. Because (almost) everyone did believe that we were the best team, I asked if we could put a plan together that would generate the results to prove that we really were. We then conducted a rigorous analysis of the current state of our business and discussed where and how we could turn things around to generate a number one performance. The team became energized by the prospect of being number one and realizing that we absolutely could get there (the plan itself was practical and realistic). Most of that team went out and executed well against that plan; some parts of the plan were modified, and, ultimately, some team members were replaced. That team went on to become the number one regional team in the country, and the incredible pride and joy that I saw in each member of that team on that achievement/recognition is something that I will never forget. That experience had an indelible impact on me of the incredible power of vision, planning, and great execution.

There are plenty of consultants who are ready, willing, and able to help with visioning. This envisioning process can be very productive—and practical—as it usually starts with an assessment of the reality of the current state of the external environment. Subsequent steps (depending on the process employed) involve assessing current organizational strengths and weaknesses, evaluating company

Going from Dead Last to Number One

When I was initially named to lead a chronically underperforming team, I was concerned. But looking back, I realize it provided me with an incredible opportunity. After all, "last-place teams" can only get better (or stay the same)!

I devoted those early days to diagnosing: spending time with my new colleagues (quietly), one-on-one listening to their customer plans, and observing them in action in front of customers. I assessed that we had some issues across the group that we could begin to address through a team strategy meeting, and then there were some individual performance issues where I coached aggressively with a goal of "shape up or ship out." The strategy session, including creating a new vision for where we were going as a team, helped in so many ways—including creating shared expectations for what each person needed to deliver. Some people eventually left the team (or were asked to leave). Several underperformers stepped up their game and performance improved—and to my surprise, some top performers got even better inspired by the new energy across the team.

culture (both current state and desired state), and discussing future goals. Through conversation, most groups can and do develop a vision statement that encompasses a more lofty and inspirational goal than "grow revenues by 20 percent." These practical goals are helpful as they can usually be broadened to something more visionary, like "become the market-leading provider of XYZ." You can also push yourself or the group to go bigger in its vision: "changing the way XYZ is delivered to better serve customers." To be effective, these big visions must be followed and supported by a practical, specific, and detailed plan for achievement.

When should you employ this unbridled optimism for visioning? This is an important question. Some leaders are naturally wired for visioning; they wake up in the morning having seen a vision for their organizations, and off they go. Others (most of us) have to work a bit harder to create the vision. Sometimes a new vision is needed in an organization. The organization might be caught in a major funk, and the leader needs to create a new vision to pull it up and out, but this should be a reasonably infrequent activity. Frankly, although creating a vision can be important to an organization, it's the practical, more regular daily, weekly, and quarterly hard work of planning and executing that puts the organization on the trajectory to achieve those visionary goals.

Although lofty visions depend on a heavy dose of unbridled optimism, we also want to touch on the optimism that leaders can bring to their everyday work and leadership of teams. In their day-to-day work, leaders must be sensitive to when people and/or teams need to focus on the practical and realistic versus the need for a shot of optimism that reinforces your belief that they can successfully get the job done. For example, I've seen high-functioning teams focused on an issue and successfully implementing plans to address it, but then a leader has a detrimental effect on the team by reviewing and revising the details of the practical plan (the untrusting micromanager) instead of employing the optimistic and trusting (after confirmation of the validity of the plan) style, which reinforces the leader's confidence in the team and allows them to implement with renewed vigor.

Generally speaking, most successful leaders tend to be optimistic, and their bias is to believe that difficult goals can be achieved. That tendency is valuable as people will follow a leader to reach an objective when they hear that the leader believes that they will achieve the goal. In their seminal research into what makes leaders credible, James Kouzes and Barry Posner (2011) identified being *forward-looking* as a key success factor. People want to follow a leader who believes that today's challenges and hard work will lead to a more successful tomorrow.

This natural optimistic tendency is helpful to organizations as these leaders genuinely tend to believe that they will prevail, and that spirit can permeate broadly throughout an organization. Leaders who show a can-do attitude toward the future inspire people to see possibilities and engage in a common purpose. When they do experience setbacks, they see them as temporary (Seligman, 1990). Compare this to people with a more negative mind-set who focus on and seem to worry more about failure. Although many would not classify Winston Churchill as an overt optimist, he maintained and communicated a belief that the allies would ultimately prevail in World War II. His belief and leadership carried Britain—and many throughout Europe—through some of the war's darkest days toward ultimate victory.

On the right side of this spectrum, it's helpful for leaders to have the ability to approach some aspects of planning practically and realistically. This is particularly true when setting budget commitments, for example. Hoping for and envisioning the best outcome is terrific—as long as you've planned and are prepared for the worst. As Cooper and Sawaf (1997, p. 124) put it, "Credible leaders are hopeful about the future yet open enough always to consider—and, if right, heed—words of caution."

There are several other examples in which leaders need to flex toward the realistic side of objective setting. If there has been a stumble on the way toward a goal, it is often helpful if the leader can get a team or individual focused on a practical, near-term goal to rebuild confidence and credibility. In some situations, this might also be an ideal time for a leader to consider creating a new vision. For example, if the setback is serious enough to render the previous vision unrealistic, then devising a new vision will be critical to reengaging and refocusing the team toward setting their sights on a new and different aspirational summit. Regularly, leaders must be able to flex fluidly across this continuum. A leader will want to practice reality testing when very excited about a project to ensure that those strong positive emotions aren't overestimating the perceived likelihood of success and unduly influencing decision-making (Stein, 2017).

Leaders often oversee groups led by other leaders. A leader's approach can also vary in response to the second-level leader's style. A visionary leader might benefit from the oversight of a more practical style to transform the vision into a tactical plan. Conversely, the more practical leader who focuses the team on only implementing the plan could benefit (as would their team) from an occasional reminder of the larger vision and objectives.

Some people mistakenly believe that managers below the CEO should be more realistic and practical and that broad vision and unbridled optimism are the purview solely of the CEO. I disagree. Some of the best young leaders that I have had the pleasure of working with create a vision within the broader vision for their team. They have bought into the grand vision and work hard with their staff to create a functional or business-unit-specific vision that supports the broader aspirations. It tends to generate incredible enthusiasm, engagement, and followership for the leader within that group.

A few years ago, I saw one of my leaders of a fairly technically oriented group putting up posters in his department related to a new vision created for the function but that I had not heard about. When I dug a little deeper, it was clear that the whole department had engaged to create this new, exciting vision and was now highly energized to implement the plan to get them there. When I asked that leader where it had all come from, he reported that the company's newly updated vision statement and a recent book that he had read had spurred him to create a specific vision and plan for his team and their function. This initiative became a powerful motivator for his group to strive to achieve the goals they had created for their specific function, which supported the broader company's achievement of goals.

As one who is constantly assessing talent, I can tell you confidently that the visioning road map isn't in the owner's manual of newly appointed C-suite executives. This is a skill that is (and can be) developed over time and is an important criterion when evaluating candidates for senior-level operating roles—and for good reason. Communicating a vision for organizational progress and growth is a common area of executive work in most organizations (Zaccaro, 2010).

As we think about the key leadership function of goal setting, it is important to determine when to approach the exercise with unbridled optimism, when to take a more realistic approach, and when to select something in between. The following are some suggestions for when to consider one or the other approach:

Optimistic ◄————————► Realistic

Consider when	*Consider when*
Making dramatic course correction	Making financial commitments
Facing difficult short-term challenges	Rebuilding credibility
Balancing another's limiting practicality	Balancing another's overoptimism
Dreaming	Breaking down vision into tactics

CHAPTER 7

FACET 4:
DECISION-MAKING

Directive ◄————————————► Delegative

All leaders make decisions. As organizations grow, decision-making becomes more decentralized, and leaders facilitate decision-making across and down the organization. If, when, and how leaders get involved in an organization's decisions is a key facet of leadership. Sometimes a leader must make a rapid decision, sometimes a decision requires more deliberation and input, and sometimes decisions shouldn't be made by the senior leader at all. Considering which skills to deploy on the continuum relates to the leader's level of knowledge, experience, and expertise on the topic at hand. This continuum consideration is further backed by research that indicates that leaders with access to information make higher-quality decisions (Henningsen, Henningsen, Jakobsen, & Borton, 2004).

Leaders come in all shapes and sizes in terms of levels of experience and knowledge. By definition, younger leaders may know less or have less experience than those they lead. At the other end of the spectrum, highly experienced leaders may have a lot of domain experience and knowledge. Regardless of where an individual is in terms of knowledge or experience, every effective leader learns when to employ their knowledge and expertise and when to step back to let individuals or teams find their own answers, to allow others to share their experience and knowledge, and to be open to let others lead.

Many of the most effective leaders I know are incredibly curious and consummate learners. How many times do we meet successful leaders and learn that they have many other interests—and that they excel at those too? I met a successful leader recently and learned that he was also an accomplished pianist. I find that some of the most skilled people have a lot of information and experiences to share, but they are usually also continually searching for additional new information, experiences, and perspectives. How do these leaders strike a balance in the process of decision-making for information conveyance versus search?

My good friend Michael is an outstanding leader. He's managed big teams and has led them to big success. We've done a lot of projects and activities together. I've observed that when he is certain of how to approach something, based on his experience, he is definitive and leaves no doubt that he knows. He can be blunt, but it's effective in getting the job done. If he is not 110 percent certain of the approach, he'll ask those around him what they think. He uses it as a personal learning opportunity, many times confirming the approach he was going to use anyway and perhaps gaining some additional perspective on why that approach is the best one. The only time I've seen him deviate from that playbook is when there is a young person involved, in which case he'll ask, "How would you come at this?" Then he gently walks the new leader through the steps he's learned from many years of experience.

When organizations are smaller, they can and normally operate in a centralized fashion where one or a small number of people make key decisions. But as they grow, that model becomes impractical and can slow things down, so a more decentralized approach is called for. In those bigger organizations, decisions will need to be made by an even larger group of people throughout the organization as it becomes more decentralized (a natural by-product of growth). Hiring and training managers throughout the

> ### When to Tell and When to Learn?
>
> *Great leaders are always learning. Even when they are in a more "directive" mode, they ask questions, listen intently, and learn.*
>
> *You may recall that in chapter 4, we discussed an especially astute leader who could easily have been one of the "no" votes on an acquisition proposal, but he was attentive to non-verbal cues and asked Evan to speak up. Even the most experienced leaders never stop learning, and in fact when/if they do, they will have initiated their own obsolescence! And remember, leaders don't have to have all the answers themselves—they just need to know how get those answers and then how to get others to follow them into action.*

organization on good decision-making skills is key to the organization's continuing success. Steve Jobs of Apple fame once said, "It doesn't make sense to hire smart people and then tell them what to do; we hire smart people so they can tell us what to do."

There's a common myth that leaders have to have *the* answer. In fact, leaders are charged with helping people get to the answer. Sometimes the best solution comes from a team member, sometimes it comes from doing outside research, and sometimes it does come from the leader—but less often than you might think. Even when the leader knows the answer, they will often not supply it but will help the group or an individual come to that very same answer on their own. I've always loved that definition of effective leadership: "Getting other people to do what you want them to do...because they want to do it." When groups and individuals come to their own (facilitated) conclusion, they are more committed to its successful implementation than when they are told to implement.

Fortunately, most leaders know many of the answers; that's why they have been given the responsibilities that have been bestowed on them. The organization does expect that they will provide effective and efficient direction. There are urgent situations when organizations depend on a rapid, definitive response from leadership. These urgent situations may take different forms. The building is on fire is certainly (and obviously) urgent, but there can also be situations that aren't so obvious but that also need to be quickly addressed. For example, if there is a strong sense of uncertainty about something that is causing broad and serious company angst, the leader likely needs to step in to provide clear and immediate direction. Many, many other times, the decision at hand is simply not that impactful, where getting the perfect decision is less important than simply making a good decision quickly.

A leader can lean into their expertise and experience when it is most effective and efficient to do so. Especially when a leader is a recognized expert, it can feel disingenuous if this expert leader defers to another person or the group. I watched a film recently on a famous fashion designer's life, an individual who had an amazing instinct to know that this material went best with that dress. The people around him expected him to be decisive on these key decisions, and a curious few asked questions in an attempt to learn. This designer did defer to other experts in his organization for other key business decisions, but he took control in the design itself. Even though many times people in an organization look to the leader as the expert (sometimes in all things), the successful leader knows better than to always supply an answer. Instead, they tap into the broader experience and expertise available across their organizations, or they simply push to search for additional information or expertise to make the best decision.

Naturally, over time a leader's expertise can become stale as their experience becomes dated or less relevant or they simply lose their magic touch (as happened with the fashion designer), but those same leaders can continue to be successful by shifting across the continuum and employing more of an open and listening approach, allowing others to offer their emerging expertise.

As we think about the leadership continuum across these facets, it's important to repeat again that there is a range across the continuum. The right place may be somewhere between the two extremes, employing more from one side of the continuum than the other, or perhaps even starting toward one side and then moving toward the other. For example, you are deciding what color to paint the office walls. Although it clearly is not a business-critical decision, you might start to the right to be open to new input. But as move-in day approaches, if there are simply too many great ideas and no consensus on how to move forward, stepping in to decide that the walls will be blue might be the most efficient and effective course. I have often found myself starting to the left, believing that I knew the answer and that it was most efficient to simply decide and move on, only to learn that I needed to shift right on the continuum as there were a variety of strong alternative opinions (and relevant experiences) from others that needed to be considered. As emotional intelligence expert Daniel Goleman (2000) has found, if you want input from valuable employees, you need to ask them what they think instead of quickly delivering your opinion.

Decision-making is something that leaders do frequently, and the approach should vary based on the specifics of the decision at hand. When considering whether to be directive, to delegate, or to do something in between, you will want to think about the following factors:

Directive ←————————→ Delegative

Consider when	Consider when
You are the obvious expert	Someone else is the expert
Urgent action is required	There is time for discussion or reflection
There is critical impact	There is low business impact
There is no obvious learning opportunity	There is an obvious learning opportunity
It is not a key decision, and you have enough information	There is lack of clarity on an issue or solution
You are open to input, but none is offered	

CHAPTER 8

FACET 5: INTENSITY

Passionate ◄━━━━━━━━━━━━━► Patient

A ll successful leaders are driven and energetic. Some leaders exhibit that energy in the way they carry themselves: moving and talking quickly, leaning in when speaking or presenting, and generally being a source of energy in a room. When researchers looked at leaders who scored at or above the ninety-ninth percentile on innovation—as measured by their peers, subordinates, and bosses in a comprehensive 360-degree feedback survey—they were described as projecting optimism, full of energy, and looking for new ideas (Zenger & Folkman, 2014).

Other great leaders are more balanced and quieter in their demeanor, but they are great leaders just the same (think the Dalai Lama, Mother Teresa, and Woodrow Wilson). Although most leaders have a natural style, the very best leaders have the ability to flex and move across this continuum, depending on the leadership challenge.

I recall years ago taking on a leadership position of underperforming product and team. When I dug into the details, I found that we had a best-in-class product and a team of many high-potential individuals. But after a string of defeats, the team appeared somewhat resigned to underperformance, and as the Vince Lombardi saying goes, "Show me a good loser, and I'll show you a loser." This team clearly needed a dose of energy, enthusiasm, and a sense of urgency. I hired a new, passionate head of sales, and with a good plan, before long we had this team and their product on a strong trajectory of sustainable growth.

I remember a vastly different situation where a team faced a difficult and complex problem. Resolution was going to require deep study, input from many experts, and careful crafting of a detailed plan for resolution. In this situation, I had to "park" my natural tendency for passion and action and step back to allow the team time and space to work their plan. It was at times frustrating for me to sit back and wait for the team to work through the long list of complex issues, but I also knew it was the right strategy to achieve the best outcome.

Although we often think of great leaders as fonts of energy and ambition, this style can be detrimental to leading organizations to success when not kept in check. When the *Apollo 13* astronauts were trapped in space in 1970 due to technical problems, there was no obvious way to bring them home. The leaders of this mission were facing what appeared to be certain doom for their astronauts. Although there were time pressures, the leader quietly supported the team of technicians, with one common refrain: failure is not an option—now back to work to figure this thing out. By calmly working through each of the many problems one by one, the team was ultimately able to bring the astronauts back to Earth safely. Had the leader been a high-energy and volatile person, without the ability to step back and let people work the problem(s), perhaps the result would have differed. In fact, research has found that executives who manage emotions well had better business outcomes than those who did not (Rosete & Ciarrochi, 2005).

Megan was an outwardly patient and paced executive whom I worked with many years ago. As I got to know Megan, I realized that a quiet intensity dwelled within this smart, aggressive person. She expressed an interest to lead a team, and although she was perhaps not an outwardly obvious candidate, I felt that Megan was worth taking a chance on. I coached and complimented her on her natural patience and balance strengths. I talked with her about developing an ability to communicate a high-energy sense of urgency at times. Megan took the coaching to heart, and

What Does Passion Look Like?

It's important for leaders to understand that passion comes in many forms. Most people naturally think of passion as loud and exuberant. And that's a natural style for many effective leaders. However, some leaders just don't/can't muster that loud exuberance in terms of their genuine leadership style—and that's OK. Passion can be shown in many ways; what is important is that the leader authentically communicates their enthusiasm, commitment, and belief in something. I knew one very effective leader who actually grew quieter and spoke more softly when he was passionate about something—and it worked. Teams leaned in to hear him, and his genuine enthusiasm and belief came through bigger and better than many others who were much louder and energetic. Over time each leader finds the passion style that is genuine and works best for them.

I'll never forget watching her at a sales meeting as she instilled an incredible sense of urgency and intensity in her team. She wasn't jumping on the table, but Megan had found a way to clearly communicate a need for her team to step up and drive hard to finish the year while staying true to her style and who she was as a leader.

Megan continued to develop and ultimately led her team to achieve outstanding results.

As most of us do, Megan had a natural tendency on the intensity scale. The key is to recognize that natural tendency, recognize the cues that another approach might be indicated, and then understand exactly how to employ the other approach (discussed later in this book). Recognizing where and when a specific situation calls for a leader to alter their natural tendencies is hard—and takes practice. Over time, experienced leaders acquire the ability to quickly "step back" and move to where they should be on the continuum to be the most effective in that situation. When considering the appropriate leadership intensity, think about the following:

Passionate ◄━━━━━━━━━━━► Patient

Consider when	*Consider when*
The problem or team requires intensity	A team or individual would benefit from space
There is fear or doubt among listeners	Problem resolution requires time
Lethargy needs to be countered	A group or individual is fragile
Urgency needs to be communicated	Things take time

CHAPTER 9

FACET 6: COMPASSION

Stern  Sensitive

Tyler was by nature a sensitive leader. In his performance reviews, I always commented on what a strong emotional quotient he had, which alludes to a measure of a manager's emotional sensitivity. He was able to read the room and the people well and to adjust his style to the particular situation and people he was dealing with. Tyler got a lot done through other people because of his sensitivity; he had great instincts on how to inspire discretionary effort and ensure strong progress on key projects. Tyler's success in this area aligns with the Center for Creative Leadership's perspective, which found that leader empathy was strongly correlated to team performance, presumably because of the importance of relationship building for leaders (Gentry, Weber, & Sadri, 2016). People loved Tyler and wanted to be on his team. He was by nature a fairly right-leaning leader on the compassion continuum.

Where Tyler and I agreed that he needed to learn to flex was in regard to acquiring an ability to sometimes be a bit more stern, insensitive, and resilient. For example, his incredible sensitivity to the personal challenges facing one person on his team, Debra, created resentment among the other members. She had missed several key meetings and was slow in responding to colleagues and customers. In the team's best interests—and for Debra—Tyler needed to be more demanding of Debra, despite an ongoing difficult personal situation. Researchers studying empathy have found that it can cloud judgment such that a leader could make a decision that affects a group of people for the benefit of an individual (Bloom, 2016).

Over several conversations, Tyler came to realize that his sensitivity toward Debra had created some problems for her and the team. By simply shifting to the left on this continuum, he was able to help Debra and the team better. He planned a one-on-one sit-down with Debra, and he let her know (more sternly than his natural style would have indicated) that her continuing absence from the team meetings was becoming an issue. He informed her that she needed to find a better solution to her ongoing personal issues at home and that the company wanted to offer whatever assistance she needed to make that happen. Tyler knew that Debra could really pull at his heartstrings with her tales of woe, and so we had prepared Tyler to be very clear with her (which he was). He ended the meeting by summing up that the current situation was unacceptable and that something had to change. They agreed to meet again for an update four days later, an important element to Tyler's something-has-to-change message to Debra.

Most of us have seen the other type of leader too—the one who is naturally more comfortable on the left side of this facet and who is fairly stern and insensitive to others and to what is going on around them. Although these types of leaders can attain a certain level of effectiveness, over time, they tend to retain only a group of fairly resilient and insensitive followers. Even though resilience can be a real virtue, lack of sensitivity across an entire team can also hurt the group. A diversity of perspectives and styles is almost always helpful, but if the team slowly weeds those other styles out, the team's homogeneity can become its biggest weakness.

Kevin had always been an incredibly dedicated and high-performing employee. When he confided to his boss that he had a personal problem at home with a sick spouse, his boss gave him significant work relief and support to deal with the issue. Once his wife was through it, Kevin bounced back and was an even more dedicated and high-performing employee. Surprised? Of course not. Flexing to being sensitive and understanding to difficult temporary personal situations can engender incredible loyalty and postissue employee work effort.

> ### Tough Love
>
> *This section touches on one of the most challenging aspects for effective leaders. The most effective leaders have—and convey—a genuine interest in the people that work for them (e.g., their families, their interests). Great leaders are genuinely interested in their employees' physical and mental well-being. Great teams enjoy spending time together, laugh together, and share pieces of their personal lives. But the leader has to draw a line and ensure that while they are "friendly," they are not "friends." Leaders need to retain certain objectivity and some level of "distance" from their direct reports. It may seem a bit crass, but always remembering that "I may have to fire this person one day" can help a leader maintain the appropriate level of distance and objectivity to manage and lead effectively.*

On the other hand, I recall a likable, high-performing employee who worked for me who began to take advantage of my understanding of her personal issues by arriving late to office meetings or giving late notice for days out of the office. I ultimately had to have a rather uncomfortable conversation about how I felt that the employee was abusing my and the company's flexibility. I was transparent with her about how some employees were starting to feel that she wasn't carrying her fair share of the work. A couple of months after that conversation, the employee left the organization for a new job, which was somewhat disappointing. However, I concluded that allowing the situation to persist would have had broader negative consequences, so I was fine with the outcome. This is a good example of flexing across the continuum from sensitive to employee issues to insensitive and ultimately resilient to the disappointment of losing a good employee.

Leaders also need to understand where they should be ideally positioned on the continuum in a group setting. For example, if there is broadscale fear or concern in a group, a leader needs to show the appropriate level of understanding—but more importantly convey a "stern" belief that the concerns can be addressed and there are better days ahead. Fear can be paralyzing for a group, and the leader's job is to focus the group on action.

When a leader steps back to think about the level of compassion that would be appropriate and most effective in a given situation, consider the following:

Stern ◄─────────────► Sensitive

Consider when	*Consider when*
The problem or team requires intensity	There is a personal or painful tragedy
There is fear among listeners	An employee needs to be heard
Lethargy needs to be countered	There is a fragile group or individual
There is a question about recoverability	Difficult failure needs to be acknowledged

CHAPTER 10

FACET 7: MOTIVATION

Self-focused ◄──────────────► Altruistic

Most people are driven by a mix of both individual (egotisti-cal?) motives and altruistic motives. Sometimes these two drivers of behavior can be at direct odds: Should I do what's best for me or what's best for the group? Leaders are also exposed to choices about self versus team. Great leaders lean more heavily right (altruism) most of the time. For example, leading a group forward to take on a courageous move that entails risk is not usually driven by a purely selfish motive. Delegating decisions to others for their development, when the instinct is that the leader knows best, is an altruistic response that's likely very good for the person delegated to and good for the organization as talent is developed and gets better.

When is it OK for leaders to be consciously selfish? Establishing a visionary goal can sometimes be a perfectly acceptable selfish act. Perhaps the team can't agree on a vision, but the leader feels strongly that their vision is what they want to achieve with the company they lead. As long as there aren't significant facts that argue that the vision is totally unachievable, it's sometimes OK for the leader to say, "Just because I want to." When some leaders set lofty visions, the people around them may think the goal is unrealistic, but the leaders then attract funding and a team that prevails. When Elon Musk decided to mass-produce a fully electric car, he didn't create that vision with input from many; instead, he "selfishly" pursued the vision that he had decided on.

Establishing a visionary goal to be number one in your business within two years might be perceived as *not* the most altruistic decision. It's going to be hard work for many people. There is a risk of disappointment if the team doesn't get there—although we could argue that these visionary leaders do have altruistic motivations in mind, knowing that the teams they lead will feel incredible pride with their eventual success and that society might even be better off. However, the leader may be accused of selfishly pursuing their vision, which, from my perspective, is acceptable and may even be necessary when chasing big goals.

Sometimes the senior leader must make the big decision. Strong leaders pull information and opinions from a variety of sources, but they ultimately feel comfortable taking responsibility for the decision—right or wrong. I have seen some really great leaders make tough decisions. In most cases, if the decision goes badly, the leader takes full and sole responsibility. When those decisions go well, those same leaders take great effort to share the responsibility with as broad a group as possible and as publicly as possible. A few years ago, my company acquired a business, but it did not go as well as we had expected. After several attempts to turn it around, I went to my board to propose a divestiture and took full and sole responsibility for the project. Several months later, when we had successfully sold the business, we celebrated and rewarded the team that led the successful divestiture of that business, which energized them to pursue further key strategic moves for the company.

Many times in my career, I have been presented with proposals for my company to support (and fund) altruistic initiatives tangentially related to (but not directly impacting) our business. These might be education programs for patients in an area of therapeutic interest for the company but not related to its products. Some of these initiatives were important in terms of their potential impact on patients, and if we did not support them, they would likely not happen. These

> ### Taking Responsibility
>
> *Regardless of underlying motivation, the best leaders take full responsibility for failure and broadly share the accolades for success. I am always amazed when I hear about executives who blame others for failure (some level of "failure," by the way, is a normal part of business). The leader's boss (e.g., manager, board of directors) can see right through a leader who blames others, and that very act calls into question other aspects of that leader's performance (was there proper oversight of their teams?). Owning up to missteps always acts as a strong validation of a leader's integrity, and dodging responsibility has the opposite effect. Taking ownership and responsibility allows the conversation to quickly pivot to a productive focus on "What did we learn?" and "What do we do now?"*

can be difficult decisions for leaders as they consider where they and their companies sit along the motivation continuum. I recall one successful initiative (which became an annual event) wherein we engaged our entire employee population to create teams and competitively raise funds to support a particularly worthy nonprofit organization. We not only supported the important work that they did for patients, but employee engagement at the company was significantly enhanced by pursuing this more altruistic initiative!

As we stated at the outset of this section, people are driven by a mix of motivations, with altruism being a fairly standard part of an effective leader's motivational set. Strong leaders challenge themselves to think through their motivations and ask if they should more consciously focus on individual/selfish motives or altruistic motives. Understanding motivations, and which side of the continuum is most appropriate for the situation, can be helpful for leaders. When thinking about motivation, consider the following:

Self-focused  Altruistic

Consider when	*Consider when*
Achieving a big goal	The team has a big goal in mind
Questioning a key personal value	The value of the greater good is high
The downside of delegation is too high	The development or buy-in value of delegating is high
There is a high-risk decision and no right answer	
The leader's health or family is at risk	

CHAPTER 11

CONTINUUM FLEX ASSESSMENT

A s you have seen so far in this book, leadership involves cali-
brating the approach to each situation. In this self-assessment
section, we encourage you to answer questions about the seven leadership facets. These self-assessments were designed to help you evaluate your natural tendencies along the continuum of the seven facets
of leadership, describe the optimal approach for these situations and
why the approach is recommended, and then guide you in focusing
your development efforts in chapter 12. We encourage you to invest
your time in these self-assessments; this is your opportunity to reflect
on your tendencies as a leader and learn how to adjust based on the
particular leadership situation. Please note that we recognize that the
term *optimal approach* in the answer section may be an overstatement
in response to these short and simple leadership scenarios.

For example, the first self-assessment focuses on the communication facet. Each section presents five scenarios, allows you to
indicate how you would respond along the continuum, and then

checks the fit of your approach to each situation versus an optimal approach. Based on your responses across several scenarios, we will help you assess whether you typically gravitate more toward the active/effective communicator profile or whether you tend to prefer taking an active listening approach. Both skills are important for a successful leader to have in their arsenal of tools to employ. If you find that you tend more to the left by taking on the active/effective communicator role, you might benefit from reviewing the tools laid out in chapter 12 under the communication facet, specifically focusing on tips for when and how to employ active listening skills.

You might want to complete all self-assessments in one sitting, or you might want to hone in on the facets that are of most interest after reading the first section of this book. Many leaders find that they can easily and naturally flex across certain facets while recognizing that others take more work. That is natural and normal. We trust that even those leaders who score perfectly will benefit from the exercise (as I did in writing them). This serves as a nice reminder of a leader's need to flex across the continuum and also when that flexing is most appropriate and necessary.

To illustrate which approach makes the most sense for each situation, we have provided an answer key for each facet.

Instructions

1) **Respond to each scenario.** Review each facet's description and then picture yourself in each scenario. What is your tendency in the situation? The more honest you are with yourself, the more useful the insights will be.

2) **Review the optimal response using the answer key.** After you answer the questions for each facet, read the answer key. Besides seeing the optimal approach to each situation, you will better understand *why* the response is preferred in this specific scenario.

3) **Notice any tendencies.** Eyeball your responses across the scenarios for which you tend to lean toward the left or the right side of the continuum. Look for these facets in the next chapter to further develop your skills.

1. Communication

Direct communicator ⟵⟶ Active listener

Consider when	*Consider when*
You are the obvious expert	Someone else is the expert
Diffusing a tense situation	Letting others sort things out
Framing a conversation	Engendering outcome ownership
Focusing a conversation	Observing and allowing others to lead

Respond to each scenario.

A. This afternoon, you are scheduled to have a one-on-one discussion with your direct report Rob. You view Rob as a high-potential employee with a bright future. However, he has been struggling lately to motivate a few people on his team. You are encouraged by Rob's willingness to improve and are eager for him to put together a plan to manage his team's challenging members. Consider the communication style that you would naturally employ to tackle this issue. Where do you tend to fall on the continuum? Circle your response.

1	2	3	4	5
Completely direct communicator	Mostly direct communicator	Somewhat direct communicator/ active listener	Mostly active listener	Completely active listener

B. As a senior leader in the company, you're joining your colleagues for the monthly senior leadership team meeting. A key topic in this meeting is how to address the recently delivered and less-than-stellar engagement survey results, which seem to have surprised the CEO, your colleagues, and yourself. Consider the communication style that you would naturally employ to tackle this issue. Where do you tend to fall on the continuum? Circle your response.

1	2	3	4	5
Completely direct communicator	Mostly direct communicator	Somewhat direct communicator/ active listener	Mostly active listener	Completely active listener

C. Your team has been working on a highly visible project that is running behind schedule. You're facilitating a meeting with your team about next steps. The challenges that the team members are facing are ones in which you have significant experience. Consider the communication style that you would naturally employ to tackle this issue. Where do you tend to fall on the continuum? Circle your response.

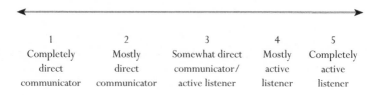

1	2	3	4	5
Completely direct communicator	Mostly direct communicator	Somewhat direct communicator/ active listener	Mostly active listener	Completely active listener

D. Two of your direct reports are known to frequently butt heads. Recently, things have become very tense and seem to be getting personal. In a team meeting, these two individuals became wrapped up in a heated back-and-forth debate that was neither productive nor healthy. Consider the communication style that you would naturally employ to tackle this issue. Where do you tend to fall on the continuum? Circle your response.

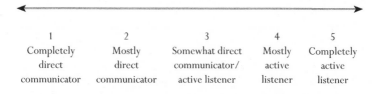

1	2	3	4	5
Completely direct communicator	Mostly direct communicator	Somewhat direct communicator/ active listener	Mostly active listener	Completely active listener

E. Jennifer, a direct report, has come to you because she is troubled by an issue she's dealing with. She tends to have good judgment and has proven to be able to work through similar issues in the past, but she does need a little time to think through challenges. Consider the communication style that you would naturally employ to tackle this issue. Where do you tend to fall on the continuum? Circle your response.

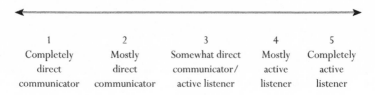

1	2	3	4	5
Completely direct communicator	Mostly direct communicator	Somewhat direct communicator/ active listener	Mostly active listener	Completely active listener

Review the optimal response using the answer key.

A. This afternoon, you are scheduled to have a one-on-one discussion with your direct report Rob. You view Rob as a high-potential employee with a bright future. However, he has been struggling lately to motivate a few people on his team. You are encouraged by Rob's willingness to improve and are eager for him to put together a plan to manage his team's challenging members.

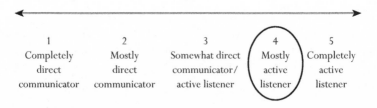

1	2	3	4	5
Completely direct communicator	Mostly direct communicator	Somewhat direct communicator/ active listener	Mostly active listener	Completely active listener

This is a situation in which you have a perfectly capable young leader working through a fairly standard leadership challenge. Rob likely needs to be listened to, needs a sounding board to bounce some ideas off, and may need some suggestions for tried-and-true tactics (that he is just unfamiliar with at this point). Rob needs to put the plan together, so a mostly active listener posture is likely the best approach.

B. As a senior leader in the company, you're joining your colleagues for the monthly senior leadership team meeting. A key topic in this meeting is how to address the recently delivered and less-than-stellar engagement survey results, which seemed to have surprised the CEO, your colleagues, and yourself.

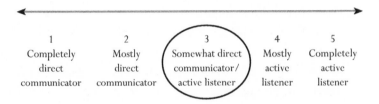

1	2	3	4	5
Completely direct communicator	Mostly direct communicator	Somewhat direct communicator/ active listener	Mostly active listener	Completely active listener

This situation calls for a balanced approach. You'll need the full team's input and buy-in for steps going forward, so a lot of listening will be required. Given that the executives were surprised by the results, there is also an opportunity for strong leadership and communication to engage the group in positive plans to address these issues.

C. Your team has been working on a highly visible project that is running behind schedule. You're facilitating a meeting with your team about next steps. The challenges that the team members are facing are ones in which you have significant experience.

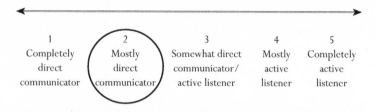

This is a moment to pull the team together and provide direct communication and leadership, especially because you have strong experience in the area. You do require team buy-in to the go-forward plan, so there will also be a need to solicit input and agreement, but this is a situation that calls for the mostly direct communicator approach.

D. Two of your direct reports are frequently known to butt heads. Recently, things have become very tense and seem to be getting personal. In a team meeting, these two individuals became wrapped up in a heated back-and-forth debate that was neither productive nor healthy.

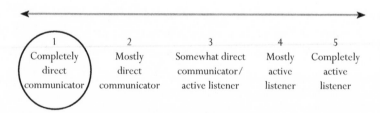

This has all the hallmarks of a situation that could go very badly. It demands strong intervention with a focus on clear and direct communication to these two individuals. If this had been the first or second instance, we might be more open to listening and input, but given that this is occurring frequently and that it appears to be escalating

(e.g., getting personal), it calls for the completely direct communication approach.

E. Jennifer, a direct report, has come to you because she is troubled by an issue she's dealing with. She tends to have good judgment and has proven to be able to work through similar issues in the past, but she does need a little time to think through challenges.

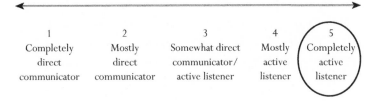

1	2	3	4	5
Completely direct communicator	Mostly direct communicator	Somewhat direct communicator/ active listener	Mostly active listener	Completely active listener

Because you know that Jennifer has good judgment, you can sit back and be a completely active listener to help her work through this issue. Coaching Jennifer on ways to come up with solutions independently, without the need for a session with you, would be beneficial for the future. Reinforcing that she has demonstrated and continues to demonstrate good judgment should help Jennifer to develop the ability to make decisions on her own and in a timelier fashion.

2. Rigidity

Principled ←————————————→ Adaptive

Consider when	*Consider when*
Relying on core beliefs to make decisions	Being receptive to having core beliefs challenged
Applying strong principles to your leadership approach	Acknowledging and respecting the different beliefs of others
Staying true to your deeply held beliefs	Remaining open to listening to and learning from others
Expecting the company to act consistently with your core beliefs	Taking a depends-on-the-facts-of-the-situation approach
Taking a strong principled position on an issue	Requesting data to correct or update your assumptions
Acting consistently across similar types of uncertainties	Delegating decisions to those with more current or relevant experience

Respond to each scenario.

A. Within a field where you have significant experience, your company is facing a serious issue that requires a decision today. Consider the rigidity style that you would naturally employ to tackle this issue. Where do you tend to fall on the continuum? Circle your response.

1	2	3	4	5
Completely principled	Mostly principled	Somewhat principled/adaptive	Mostly adaptive	Completely adaptive

B. You are having an informal lunch with a new young manager in the company, and he describes a project that he is working on. He specifically mentions a problem that he is confronting. Consider the rigidity style that you would naturally employ to tackle this issue. Where do you tend to fall on the continuum? Circle your response.

1	2	3	4	5
Completely principled	Mostly principled	Somewhat principled/adaptive	Mostly adaptive	Completely adaptive

C. A direct report runs by you how he is trying to encourage even better performance from one of his key managers. He seems to be employing a reasonable coaching approach. Consider the rigidity style that you would naturally employ to tackle this issue. Where do you tend to fall on the continuum? Circle your response.

1	2	3	4	5
Completely principled	Mostly principled	Somewhat principled/adaptive	Mostly adaptive	Completely adaptive

D. This scenario is continued from the previous one, but this is the third conversation you have had with this executive about this issue, and he continues to use the same coaching approach. Consider the rigidity style that you would naturally employ to tackle this issue. Where do you tend to fall on the continuum? Circle your response.

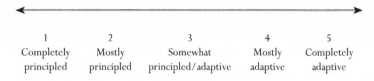

1	2	3	4	5
Completely principled	Mostly principled	Somewhat principled/adaptive	Mostly adaptive	Completely adaptive

E. You are meeting with a team about the location of a three-day off-site meeting that is three months away. You ask for ideas, and with none forthcoming, you propose two locations that the group readily agrees to. Consider the rigidity style that you would naturally employ to tackle this issue. Where do you tend to fall on the continuum? Circle your response.

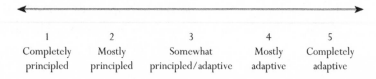

1	2	3	4	5
Completely principled	Mostly principled	Somewhat principled/adaptive	Mostly adaptive	Completely adaptive

Review the optimal response using the answer key.

A. Within a field where you have significant experience, your company is facing a serious issue that requires a decision today.

Given the urgent need for this decision, the fact that it is a serious issue, and that you have significant experience, the most appropriate strategy would be a direct and experience-based approach (yours).

B. You are having an informal lunch with a new young manager in the company, and he describes a project that he is working on. He specifically mentions a problem that he is confronting.

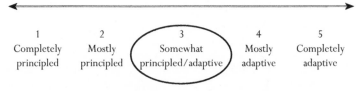

This appears to be a perfect mentoring opportunity. It would be ideal to have a relatively open and flexible approach with this young manager that is balanced by giving some structure to the discussion. If you approach the conversation in too structured a fashion, there is a risk of losing the benefits of flexibly working through the issue and narrowing down the approach. Discussing the issue with no structure at all risks not providing a structure for dealing with this type of issue in the future.

C. A direct report runs by you how he is trying to encourage even better performance from one of his key managers. He seems to be employing a reasonable coaching approach.

This type of situation can be a great opportunity to do a lot of listening and relatively open questioning. The manager is employing a reasonable approach, so there is no need to provide a new structure to address the problem.

D. This scenario is continued from the previous one, but this is the third conversation you have had with this executive about this issue, and he continues to use the same coaching approach.

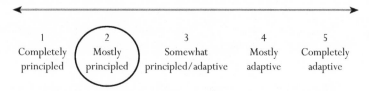

In this situation, the approach needs to change. The original approach appeared reasonable, but now it's clear that a different strategy must be employed. The manager's role here is to help this leader move on from an approach that is not working and to provide a new approach to the issue that would be most helpful. The adaptive approach hasn't worked to help this manager resolve the issue. It's time to flex across the continuum to a more principled approach.

E. You are meeting with a team about the location of a three-day off-site meeting that is three months away. You ask for ideas, and with none forthcoming, you propose two locations that the group readily agrees to.

1	2	3	4	5
Completely principled	Mostly principled	Somewhat principled/adaptive	Mostly adaptive	Completely adaptive

A meeting's location is (almost) never important and therefore does not require a rigid approach. This group is not communicating much, and a noncritical issue is a perfect opportunity to draw the group out and encourage them to discuss and decide.

3. Goal Setting

Optimistic ⟵————————⟶ Realistic

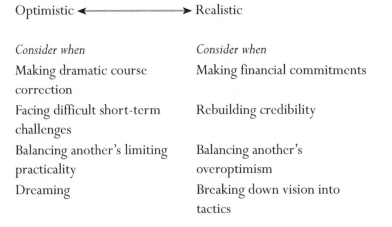

Consider when	*Consider when*
Making dramatic course correction	Making financial commitments
Facing difficult short-term challenges	Rebuilding credibility
Balancing another's limiting practicality	Balancing another's overoptimism
Dreaming	Breaking down vision into tactics

Respond to each scenario.

A. You are kicking off the annual budgeting process, and it's time to give your team some broad direction in preparation for their revenue and expense forecasts for the next fiscal year. Consider the goal-setting style that you would naturally employ to tackle this issue. Where do you tend to fall on the continuum? Circle your response.

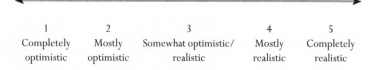

1	2	3	4	5
Completely optimistic	Mostly optimistic	Somewhat optimistic/ realistic	Mostly realistic	Completely realistic

B. One of your managers, Miguel, has come to you for advice. He is planning a two-day off-site meeting with his team to put together a five-year plan. Miguel is very practical, and so he has a series of spreadsheets with key financials already prepared that he is proposing to have the group fill in as a team. He wants to know what you think of the approach. Consider the goal-setting style that you would naturally employ to tackle this issue. Where do you tend to fall on the continuum? Circle your response.

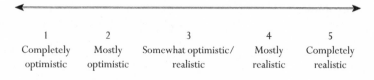

1	2	3	4	5
Completely optimistic	Mostly optimistic	Somewhat optimistic/ realistic	Mostly realistic	Completely realistic

C. You've just taken on a new team/function that has been a chronically underperforming unit. You don't yet understand the details of the function, but as you walk into the room to meet the team, it's pretty obvious that they are a disheartened group. Consider the goal-setting style that you would naturally employ to tackle this issue. Where do you tend to fall on the continuum? Circle your response.

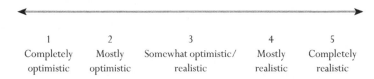

1	2	3	4	5
Completely optimistic	Mostly optimistic	Somewhat optimistic/ realistic	Mostly realistic	Completely realistic

D. One of your department heads has arranged for a strategic planning session with her team. Eva, the department leader, comes to you to get your input on her first few slides. The slides lay out the current situation and then the big vision for the future. Specifically, she wants to challenge the group to become the number one brand (by market share) in its category, which you believe is possible (although challenging). Once she gets buy-in on the vision, she says that she will challenge the group to map out the tactical plans that will support the vision's achievement. Consider the goal-setting style that you would naturally employ to tackle this issue. Where do you tend to fall on the continuum? Circle your response.

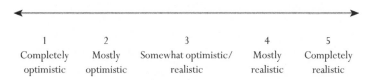

1	2	3	4	5
Completely optimistic	Mostly optimistic	Somewhat optimistic/ realistic	Mostly realistic	Completely realistic

E. John has established great followership. His team loves him, works hard for him, and embraces the annual challenge of changing the world in some big way that John inspires them with every January. Unfortunately, they just don't seem ever to meet the bigger and longer-term (or the shorter-term) objectives. John comes to you, as optimistic as ever for the start of the New Year, for some input on his upcoming team meeting. Consider the goal-setting style that you would naturally employ to tackle this issue. Where do you tend to fall on the continuum? Circle your response.

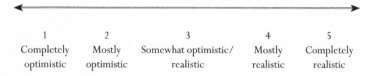

1	2	3	4	5
Completely optimistic	Mostly optimistic	Somewhat optimistic/ realistic	Mostly realistic	Completely realistic

Review the optimal response using the answer key.

A. You are kicking off the annual budgeting process, and it's time to give your team some broad direction in preparation for their revenue and expense forecasts for the next fiscal year.

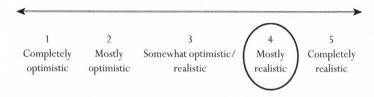

1	2	3	4	5
Completely optimistic	Mostly optimistic	Somewhat optimistic/ realistic	Mostly realistic	Completely realistic

The annual budgeting process requires a fairly practical approach, where managers and teams should be encouraged to be realistic (not to overreach or overcommit). The ideal approach would be mostly realistic, as there should be some aspirational element as teams think through plans for next year. If an operational plan is too practical, the team may not take any risks or try new things—and perhaps miss the chance for big gains. As a leader once said to me, the annual planning process should be 90 percent perspiration (hard work) and 10 percent inspiration.

B. One of your managers, Miguel, has come to you for advice. He is planning a two-day off-site meeting with his team to put together a five-year plan. Miguel is very practical, and so he has a series of spreadsheets with key financials already prepared that he is proposing to have the group fill in as a team. He wants to know what you think of the approach.

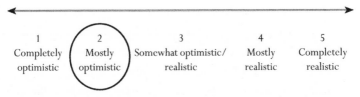

1	2	3	4	5
Completely optimistic	Mostly optimistic	Somewhat optimistic/ realistic	Mostly realistic	Completely realistic

To balance Miguel's practical (too practical?) approach, the best strategy here is to provide some more optimistic guidance around visioning. Approaching a longer-range plan (≥ five years) first requires that you establish some longer-term objectives with your team. Longer-term objectives tend to be less specific than near-term objectives, or, at a minimum, the longer-term view should start with broader goals that may later be refined into more specific, measurable goals. Asking Miguel questions about how he would like his team/function to look in five years is recommended. For example, what big things might they have accomplished in the last five years? How are they positioned in the industry versus five years ago? What would Miguel be most proud of looking back at the five-year journey that he is mapping out now?

C.   You've just taken on a new team/function that has been a chronically underperforming unit. You don't yet understand the details of the function, but as you walk into the room to meet the team, it's pretty obvious that they are a disheartened group.

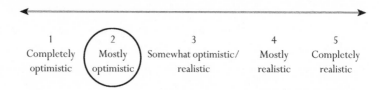

1	2	3	4	5
Completely optimistic	Mostly optimistic	Somewhat optimistic/ realistic	Mostly realistic	Completely realistic

Because you don't yet have a detailed understanding of the function or the people, it is hard (and likely not appropriate) for you to address any practical aspects of the business. The disheartened group likely needs strong leadership, optimism for a turnaround, and a vision for what could be, followed by an operational plan to make it a reality. At this point, the leader's best approach is to convey some nonspecific optimism for the team and its business prospects and the leader's enthusiasm to jump in with the team's support. It is likely inappropriate to get too specific about vision at this stage until you have had more time to assess the function, its issues and opportunities, and its people.

D.   One of your department heads has arranged for a strategic planning session with her team. Eva, the department leader, comes to you to get your input on her first few slides. The slides lay out the current situation and then a big vision for the future. Specifically, she wants to challenge the group to become the number one brand (by market share) in its category, which you believe is possible (although challenging). Once she gets buy-in on the vision, she says that she will challenge the group to map out the tactical plans that will support the vision's achievement.

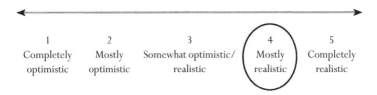

1	2	3	4	5
Completely optimistic	Mostly optimistic	Somewhat optimistic/ realistic	Mostly realistic	Completely realistic

Eva has done a nice job of setting up for a productive strategic planning session. Her vision to become the market leader is aspirational but not unrealistic. Eva is off to a good start, and there does not appear to be a need for significant course correction. She seems to recognize the need for vision to be supported by a more specific tactical plan, and so this conversation can likely be approached in a more balanced style. Eva hasn't mentioned establishing mile markers on the journey toward market leadership, and so perhaps this is an area to encourage her to include in team planning. On that more practical level, you could ask Eva and the team how they will know whether they are on track to reach the big market leadership goal as they implement their plan.

E. John has established great followership. His team loves him, works hard for him, and embraces the annual challenge of changing the world in some big way that John inspires them with every January. Unfortunately, they just don't seem to ever meet the bigger and longer-term (or the shorter-term) objectives. John comes to you, as optimistic as ever for the start of the New Year, for some input on his upcoming team meeting.

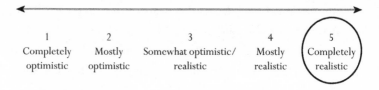

1	2	3	4	5
Completely optimistic	Mostly optimistic	Somewhat optimistic/ realistic	Mostly realistic	Completely realistic

John needs a strong dose of realistic practicality. He and his team must translate the grand vision into practical near-term goals that are achievable and that are supported by strategies and tactical plans. This plan must include very near-term (quarterly/monthly) forecasting so that progress can be carefully tracked to understand if the strategies or plans are achieving their intended result and if not, to understand further if they are the wrong strategies or tactics or perhaps poor execution.

4. Decision-Making

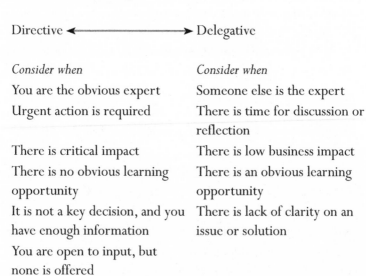

Directive ◄─────────► Delegative

Consider when	*Consider when*
You are the obvious expert	Someone else is the expert
Urgent action is required	There is time for discussion or reflection
There is critical impact	There is low business impact
There is no obvious learning opportunity	There is an obvious learning opportunity
It is not a key decision, and you have enough information	There is lack of clarity on an issue or solution
You are open to input, but none is offered	

Respond to each scenario.

A. Kayla has asked you to observe her team as they brainstorm a challenging business issue (for which there is no apparent right answer). The group has come up with several reasonable approaches, and Kayla is about to continue facilitating the meeting. Still, she pauses to see if you want to step in to make a decision. Consider the decision-making style that you would naturally employ to tackle this issue. Where do you tend to fall on the continuum? Circle your response.

1	2	3	4	5
Completely directive	Mostly directive	Somewhat directive/delegative	Mostly delegative	Completely delegative

B. A junior-level employee has come to you for a decision on the lunch menu for an upcoming meeting. You had given this employee some guidance in the last discussion and had encouraged them to make the decision. They are back and are clearly uncomfortable making the decision, and you are late for a meeting. Consider the decision-making style that you would naturally employ to tackle this issue. Where do you tend to fall on the continuum? Circle your response.

1	2	3	4	5
Completely directive	Mostly directive	Somewhat directive/delegative	Mostly delegative	Completely delegative

C. Erik is a talented manager who has good potential to develop. He has been meeting with you to create a new strategy for the program he is working on. Over the course of a couple of meetings, he has refined his thinking and has come up with a nice straw man to take to his team. In this meeting, he seems to want you to make the decision, and he asks specifically, "So, what's your decision?" Consider the decision-making style that you would naturally employ to tackle this issue. Where do you tend to fall on the continuum? Circle your response.

1	2	3	4	5
Completely directive	Mostly directive	Somewhat directive/delegative	Mostly delegative	Completely delegative

D. You are head of the pricing team at your company. Although you are an expert in the field, you manage a team of people who are also very experienced. On one particular pricing issue, the team has studied various possible strategies, and now it comes to you for a final decision. The meeting is scheduled for an hour-long discussion, and you have a list of questions for the team. Consider the decision-making style that you would naturally employ to tackle this issue. Where do you tend to fall on the continuum? Circle your response.

1	2	3	4	5
Completely directive	Mostly directive	Somewhat directive/delegative	Mostly delegative	Completely delegative

E. As president of the division, you are responsible for submitting next year's budget by the fifteenth of this month. The budgets have all been presented, and now the management team is discussing the various changes that could be made. There appears to be good general alignment (and some minor disagreements). The budget needs to be submitted in the next forty-eight hours. Consider the decision-making style that you would naturally employ to tackle this issue. Where do you tend to fall on the continuum? Circle your response.

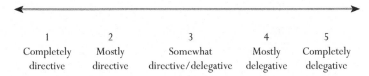

1	2	3	4	5
Completely directive	Mostly directive	Somewhat directive/delegative	Mostly delegative	Completely delegative

Review the optimal response using the answer key.

A. Kayla has asked you to observe her team as they brainstorm a challenging business issue (where there is no apparent right answer). The group has come up with several reasonable approaches, and Kayla is about to continue facilitating the meeting. Still, she pauses to see if you want to step in to make a decision.

1	2	3	4	5
Completely directive	Mostly directive	Somewhat directive/delegative	Mostly delegative	Completely delegative

Brainstorming sessions, by definition, are forums in which managers should generally refrain from making decisions. In this situation, Kayla has invited the manager to observe the team brainstorming (and has not been asked to make decisions). Kayla seems to be handling the session well, and so the most appropriate response would be for the manager to continue to simply observe and delegate. If the manager did have feedback or insights, it would be best to give those to Kayla one-on-one so as not to undercut the team's understanding that Kayla is leading the group (and not her boss).

B. A junior-level employee has come to you for a decision on the lunch menu for an upcoming meeting. You had given this employee some guidance in the last discussion and had encouraged them to make the decision. They are back and are clearly uncomfortable making the decision, and you are late for a meeting.

This is one of those simple decisions that good leaders don't stew over; they make the decision and move on. Although in this case the manager did attempt to delegate the decision to this lower-level employee (a nice development opportunity for this employee), the employee did not take the opportunity. This is an easy one; make the decision and get to your next meeting.

C. Erik is a talented manager who has good potential to develop. He has been meeting with you to create a new strategy for the program he is working on. Over the course of a couple of meetings, he has refined his thinking and has come up with a nice strawman to take to his team. In this meeting, he seems to want you to make the decision, and he asks specifically, "So, what's your decision?"

1	2	3	4	5
Completely directive	Mostly directive	Somewhat directive/delegative	Mostly delegative	Completely delegative

Good leaders resist the temptation to make the decision. Keep pushing to delegate and allow this young manager to own his recommendation. Although it would be appropriate for Erik's manager to take a position and reinforce why Erik's approach makes sense, the right strategy is to continue delegating. As part of the conversation, ask Eric, "Why are you uncomfortable making this decision on your own?" Sometimes people worry that they may be wrong. In those cases, exploring the worst that could happen can be informative. Here is another useful question to ask: "What does 'I am wrong' really look like?"

D. You are head of the pricing team at your company. Although you are an expert in the field, you manage a team of people who are also very experienced. On one particular pricing issue, the team has studied various possible strategies, and now it comes to you for a final decision. The meeting is scheduled for an hour-long discussion, and you have a list of questions for the team.

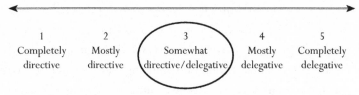

This is one of those situations in which a more balanced approach is likely the optimal answer. You are an expert; your knowledge and experience should be employed to ensure that the most appropriate strategy is selected. However, the group presenting to you is also made up of experienced (perhaps somewhat less than you) individuals whose expertise should be respected and acknowledged——and perhaps further developed through the upcoming discussion.

E. As president of the division, you are responsible for submitting next year's budget by the fifteenth of this month. The budgets have all been presented, and now the management team is discussing the various changes that could be made. There appears to be good general alignment (and some minor disagreements). The budget needs to be submitted in the next forty-eight hours.

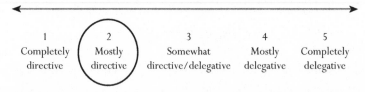

The budgets are in, there has been good discussion, and there is good alignment among management. The best approach at this time, especially with forty-eight hours to go, is to wrap things up by being mostly directive. There may be a few items to tie up by further discussion, but

at this point, the team needs strong direction and decisions. "We are clear on the top eight budget items, so those items are closed. I'd like to delegate resolution of the final two items to Manuela, who will get some additional input and will let the group know where those two items land by end of day tomorrow."

5. Intensity

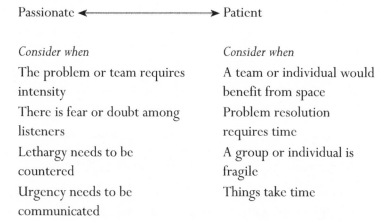

Passionate ⬅——————➡ Patient

Consider when	*Consider when*
The problem or team requires intensity	A team or individual would benefit from space
There is fear or doubt among listeners	Problem resolution requires time
Lethargy needs to be countered	A group or individual is fragile
Urgency needs to be communicated	Things take time

A. Amanda manages a very capable team that is tackling an important project for the company: a project with big potential impact and significant complexities. Amanda is a hard-charging executive, and in your weekly one-on-one, she expresses some frustration with the speed at which the project is progressing. In your experience, the project is moving forward at a good pace. Consider the intensity style that you would naturally employ to tackle this issue. Where do you tend to fall on the continuum? Circle your response.

1	2	3	4	5
Completely passionate	Mostly passionate	Somewhat passionate/patient	Mostly patient	Completely patient

B. A competitor has just launched a product similar to your top-selling product. This was a surprise, and you've called an 8:00 a.m. meeting with the commercial team to discuss the go-forward plan. Consider the intensity style that you would naturally employ to tackle this issue. Where do you tend to fall on the continuum? Circle your response.

1	2	3	4	5
Completely passionate	Mostly passionate	Somewhat passionate/patient	Mostly patient	Completely patient

C. Arthur was a popular leader, but he abruptly resigned from his position recently. Fortunately, one member of his team, Christine, has been preparing to take on more responsibility and is ready to step into this role. Her promotion has been announced, the team has responded well, and they are all preparing for the two-day annual planning session next week. You are prepared to open the two-day meeting to show your strong support of Christine. She has just stopped by to go through her (solid) plans for the two-day session and was surprised that you were planning to attend. She feels strongly that your presence would undermine her new authority, and while she expresses appreciation for your support, she politely asks that you step back and let her lead her new team solo. As you think about it, you have total confidence in Christine, but you'd love to be present to help. Consider the intensity style that you would naturally employ to tackle this issue. Where do you tend to fall on the continuum? Circle your response.

1	2	3	4	5
Completely passionate	Mostly passionate	Somewhat passionate/patient	Mostly patient	Completely patient

D. You have been asked to address the project alpha group. This group has recently faced several setbacks, as technical hurdles on this project have been more daunting than originally foreseen. Morale has suffered, and last week, two of the most senior engineers resigned. You have dug deep into the specifics and are convinced that the group will succeed in overcoming the technical hurdles with another six months of hard work. Consider the intensity style that you would naturally employ to tackle this issue. Where do you tend to fall on the continuum? Circle your response.

1	2	3	4	5
Completely passionate	Mostly passionate	Somewhat passionate/patient	Mostly patient	Completely patient

E. You have been asked to address a group of leaders from a division that has been a solid performer for the last three years but that never seems to break out. For each of the three years, they have established stretch goals that they don't reach. However, they do consistently deliver solid top- and bottom-line performance. The new head of the division has asked you to open the meeting to get them fired up but warns that there's a bit of skepticism after another on-target performance year. Consider the intensity style that you would naturally employ to tackle this issue. Where do you tend to fall on the continuum? Circle your response.

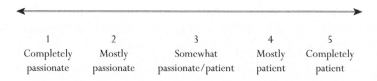

1	2	3	4	5
Completely passionate	Mostly passionate	Somewhat passionate/patient	Mostly patient	Completely patient

Review the optimal response using the answer key.

A. Amanda manages a very capable team that is tackling an important project for the company: a project with big potential impact and significant complexities. Amanda is a hard-charging executive, and in your weekly one-on-one, she expresses some frustration with the speed at which the project is progressing. In your experience, the project is moving forward at a good pace.

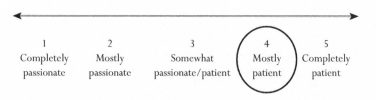

1	2	3	4	5
Completely passionate	Mostly passionate	Somewhat passionate/patient	Mostly patient	Completely patient

This is great opportunity to provide some balance to Amanda's normally hard-charging approach. This is a high-performing group that, based on your experience, is tackling this project at the right pace, and so it will be important to approach this conversation in a mostly balanced and patient style. Amanda may feel that you are not listening or don't understand if you exhibit too much patience. Your role is to support Amanda's intensity and offer some balance so that she does not push her group at an unrealistic or unproductive pace in tackling this important project.

B. A competitor has just launched a product similar to your top-selling product. This was a surprise, and you've called an 8:00 a.m. meeting with the commercial team to discuss the go-forward plan.

1	2	3	4	5
Completely passionate	Mostly passionate	Somewhat passionate/patient	Mostly patient	Completely patient

This is one of those leadership moments in which a strong leader must show up with a high level of energy and passion. This is a very important issue facing the company, and so anything less than maximum intensity won't do. The leader does not want to appear panicked but instead needs to communicate a high energy and focus commensurate with the threat's seriousness. A near-term action plan should result from this meeting, with clear next steps and close follow-up.

C. Arthur was a popular leader, but he abruptly resigned from his position recently. Fortunately, one member of his team,

Christine, has been preparing to take on more responsibility and is ready to step into this role. Her promotion has been announced, the team has responded well, and they are all preparing for the two-day annual planning session next week. You are prepared to open the two-day meeting to show your strong support of Christine. She has just stopped by to go through her (solid) plans for the two-day session and was surprised that you were planning to attend. She feels strongly that your presence would undermine her new authority, and while she expresses appreciation for your support, she politely asks that you step back and let her lead her new team solo. As you think about it, you have total confidence in Christine, but you'd love to be present to help.

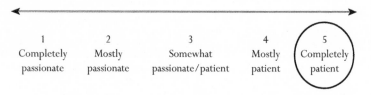

1	2	3	4	5
Completely passionate	Mostly passionate	Somewhat passionate/patient	Mostly patient	Completely patient

This circumstance is not uncommon; a leader is ready to step in or step up with intensity, only to discover that the leaders below them—in whom they have total confidence—would prefer that they be allowed to lead, with a (sometimes subtle) request that the senior leader exhibit patience and step back. Although this vignette could also appear under the decision-making facet referencing delegation, we have included it here to remind readers that sometimes a leader's natural passion can also get in the way of healthy delegation. This is a good example of when the leader has every reason to step back and allow this new young leader to lead.

D. You have been asked to address the project alpha group. This group has recently faced several setbacks, as technical hurdles on this project have been more daunting than originally foreseen. Morale has suffered, and last week, two of the most senior engineers resigned. You have dug deep into the specifics and are convinced that the group will succeed in overcoming the technical hurdles with another six months of hard work.

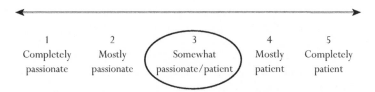

1	2	3	4	5
Completely passionate	Mostly passionate	Somewhat passionate/patient	Mostly patient	Completely patient

This is one of those delicate situations that likely needs an equal dose of positive high energy and passion and a show of balance and patience to a somewhat demoralized and fragile group. In this instance, the leader's job is to empathetically acknowledge where the project is (and some of the challenges faced along the way) while injecting a strong dose of energy and enthusiasm for the road ahead and the team's ultimate success, which is achievable with continued hard work. Too much empathy will not help pull the group out of its current funk, but too much passion could exacerbate the current negative sentiment.

E. You have been asked to address a group of leaders from a division that has been a solid performer for the last three years but that never seems to break out. For each of the three years, they have established stretch goals that they don't reach. However, they do consistently deliver solid top- and bottom-line performance. The new head of the division has asked you to open the meeting to get them fired up but warns that there's a bit of skepticism after another on-target performance year.

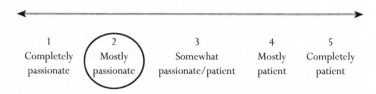

1	2	3	4	5
Completely passionate	Mostly passionate	Somewhat passionate/patient	Mostly patient	Completely patient

This situation calls for a mostly high-energy/passionate style, tempered with the balance appropriate when addressing a skeptical crowd. You would want to do more work to understand why the division hasn't been able to break out, including asking questions such as these: How do we define breakout performance? Is it realistic? Are the leaders getting the resources needed to deliver the above plan performance? So many more details would be needed before you jump up on that stage, but stylistically, it would be best to approach this meeting with division leadership in a mostly passionate fashion.

6. Compassion

Stern ←——————————→ Sensitive

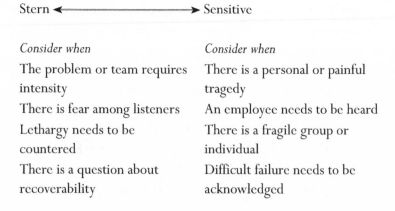

Consider when	*Consider when*
The problem or team requires intensity	There is a personal or painful tragedy
There is fear among listeners	An employee needs to be heard
Lethargy needs to be countered	There is a fragile group or individual
There is a question about recoverability	Difficult failure needs to be acknowledged

A. Sean returns from a holiday break with news that his mother has been diagnosed with a serious illness. Sean's performance over the last year has been satisfactory but not stellar. He meets expectations but doesn't exert the extra effort to overachieve in any area. He ends his vacation summary by saying, "I'll probably need to come in late or leave early a few days a week as my mother recovers." Consider the compassion style that you would naturally employ to tackle this issue. Where do you tend to fall on the continuum? Circle your response.

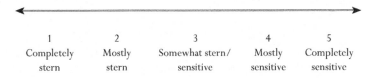

1	2	3	4	5
Completely stern	Mostly stern	Somewhat stern/ sensitive	Mostly sensitive	Completely sensitive

B. A competitor has publicly accused the company of falsifying accounting records. You have confirmed that this is untrue, and your accounting firm has validated your belief. This particular competitor is on the verge of bankruptcy, and this seems like a desperate attempt to discredit your company in the eyes of customers. In a company meeting, an employee asks about the issue. Consider the compassion style that you would naturally employ to tackle this issue. Where do you tend to fall on the continuum? Circle your response.

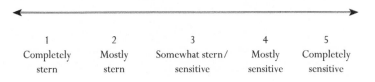

1	2	3	4	5
Completely stern	Mostly stern	Somewhat stern/ sensitive	Mostly sensitive	Completely sensitive

C. Lauren reports to you that a key initiative has been a failure. This initiative could have had a big payoff, but it had a high risk of failure, which was relatively inexpensive. Although you are somewhat disappointed, there is nothing that the team could have done better, and you are happy to move on. However, Lauren is clearly upset about the failure. Consider the compassion style that you would naturally employ to tackle this issue. Where do you tend to fall on the continuum? Circle your response.

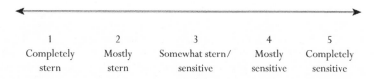

1	2	3	4	5
Completely stern	Mostly stern	Somewhat stern/ sensitive	Mostly sensitive	Completely sensitive

D. Mark comes to you somewhat dispirited. He has been leading his team through a difficult transition, and although they are making progress, it is behind expectations. He appears sad and frustrated. He wants to get things back on track but is struggling with the approach. Consider the compassion style that you would naturally employ to tackle this issue. Where do you tend to fall on the continuum? Circle your response.

1	2	3	4	5
Completely stern	Mostly stern	Somewhat stern/ sensitive	Mostly sensitive	Completely sensitive

E. An employee comes to you because she has just learned that Morgan, an accounting department employee, has revealed that her husband died unexpectedly over the weekend. She asks you if the company would be willing to send flowers. Consider the compassion style that you would naturally employ to tackle this issue. Where do you tend to fall on the continuum? Circle your response.

1	2	3	4	5
Completely stern	Mostly stern	Somewhat stern/ sensitive	Mostly sensitive	Completely sensitive

Review the optimal response using the answer key.

A. Sean returns from a holiday break with news that his mother has been diagnosed with a serious illness. Sean's performance over the last year has been satisfactory but not stellar. He meets expectations but doesn't exert the extra effort to overachieve in any area. He ends his vacation summary by saying, "I'll probably need to come in late or leave early a few days a week as my mother recovers."

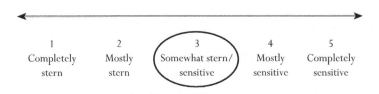

1	2	3	4	5
Completely stern	Mostly stern	Somewhat stern/ sensitive	Mostly sensitive	Completely sensitive

It would be appropriate to express some empathy about Sean's mother's health. However, this situation deserves a more balanced approach, with some level of sternness and insensitivity to Sean, considering the impact that his presaged out-of-office expectations will have on his team and the company. Responding too sternly would likely create negativity with Sean (and other colleagues he tells), but being too sensitive leaves the impression that his expected absences are acceptable. This might not be the time to be too specific about a solution, and so an approach express-ing concern about Sean's mother should be balanced with a comment about how you are also concerned about the effect his expected absence will have on his colleagues and the company.

B.   A competitor has publicly accused the company of falsifying accounting records. You have confirmed that this is untrue, and your accounting firm has validated your belief. This particular competitor is on the verge of bankruptcy, and this seems like a desperate attempt to discredit your company in the eyes of customers. In a company meeting, an employee asks about the issue.

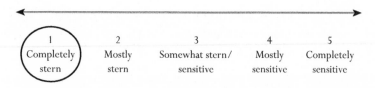

1	2	3	4	5
Completely stern	Mostly stern	Somewhat stern/ sensitive	Mostly sensitive	Completely sensitive

This is one of those situations in which a leader has every right—indeed, an obligation—to be strong and stern. Employees have heard the accusation; a seed of doubt has been planted, and they are look-ing for leadership to respond. The response should be clear, strong, and definitive. Although it is unfortunate that a competitor is facing a difficult potential bankruptcy situation, this is no time to show any level of compassion for its fate.

C. Lauren reports to you that a key initiative has been a failure. This initiative could have had a big payoff, but it had a high risk of failure, which was relatively inexpensive. Although you are somewhat disappointed, there is nothing that the team could have done better, and you are happy to move on. However, Lauren is clearly upset about the failure.

1	2	3	4	5
Completely stern	Mostly stern	Somewhat stern/ sensitive	Mostly sensitive	Completely sensitive

In this situation, just listening will likely be of assistance to Lauren. Failure, no matter how inconsequential, can be challenging for leaders, and they need to work through it. This is a sign of a tough and competitive individual. As leaders mature, they can move more quickly through minor setbacks, but it is a learned skill. In this case, listening empathetically can be helpful, with perhaps a reinforcement of the failure's low cost. The goal of this discussion is to help Lauren move on as quickly as possible.

D. Mark comes to you somewhat dispirited. He has been leading his team through a difficult transition, and although they are making progress, it is behind expectations. He appears sad and frustrated. He wants to get things back on track but is struggling with the approach.

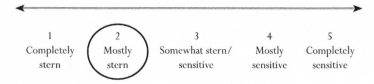

1	2	3	4	5
Completely stern	Mostly stern	Somewhat stern/ sensitive	Mostly sensitive	Completely sensitive

Although you can acknowledge Mark's frustration, moving the conversation insensitively to evaluating practical approaches to getting things back on track would be most helpful. As a team leader, Mark should be made to understand that his current dispirited demeanor could be a part of the problem. A leader's visible pessimism about achieving goals can become a self-fulfilling prophecy for the group.

E. An employee comes to you to because she has just learned that Morgan, an employee in the accounting department, has revealed that her husband died unexpectedly over the weekend. She asks you if the company would be willing to send flowers.

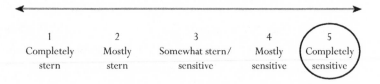

1	2	3	4	5
Completely stern	Mostly stern	Somewhat stern/ sensitive	Mostly sensitive	Completely sensitive

In situations of personal tragedy, the correct response is always to be completely sensitive. Although these situations can seem so straightforward to many people, sometimes a natural tendency to be practical can mask the requisite empathy—and be misinterpreted. Although it might be practical in this situation, for example, to pause and wait to hear what the family would prefer, a hesitant response might be misread by this employee (and others) as insensitive and not caring about the colleague's tragedy. The best response would be to simply express appropriate empathy for the colleague's loss and agree with the employee's gesture of condolence.

7. Motivation

Self-focused ←——————————→ Altruistic

Consider when	*Consider when*
Achieving a big goal	The team has a big goal in mind
Questioning a key personal value	The value of the greater good is high
The downside of delegation is too high	The development or buy-in value of delegating is high
There is a high-risk decision and no right answer	
The leader's health or family is at risk	

Respond to each scenario.

A. You are at an off-site with your executive team to develop a vision for the go-forward division that you lead. The group has generally coalesced around a big vision that is slightly less ambitious than you had hoped. Despite your cajoling, the team is enthusiastically dug into their vision statement. Consider the motivation style that you would naturally employ to tackle this issue. Where do you tend to fall on the continuum? Circle your response.

1	2	3	4	5
Completely self-focused	Mostly self-focused	Somewhat self-focused/altruistic	Mostly altruistic	Completely altruistic

B. Your company is facing a series of significant issues you are working through in some evening sessions with your executive team. On the home front, you have recently felt the need to spend more time with your twelve-year-old, who is struggling a bit in school. You've decided you can absolutely do both. Consider the motivation style that you would naturally employ to tackle this issue. Where do you tend to fall on the continuum? Circle your response.

1	2	3	4	5
Completely self-focused	Mostly self-focused	Somewhat self-focused/altruistic	Mostly altruistic	Completely altruistic

C. The company is facing a big decision to sell a division. There is significant disagreement among the management team as to whether this is the right decision; some are strongly in favor, while some are strongly opposed. There are good arguments on both sides. You have never really believed in the potential of this business and are in favor of selling. Consider the motivation style that you would naturally employ to tackle this issue. Where do you tend to fall on the continuum? Circle your response.

1	2	3	4	5
Completely self-focused	Mostly self-focused	Somewhat self-focused/altruistic	Mostly altruistic	Completely altruistic

D. At your annual health checkup, your physician strongly advises that you dedicate some time to physical exercise. You tell her how demanding your job is and how you get in early and work late to be available to your teams when they need you. Your physician suggests blocking two early mornings each week as untouchable, during which you would start a modest exercise regimen. It seems possible, but you're not sure. Consider the motivation style that you would naturally employ to tackle this issue. Where do you tend to fall on the continuum? Circle your response.

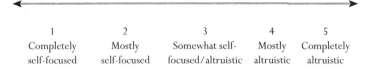

1	2	3	4	5
Completely self-focused	Mostly self-focused	Somewhat self-focused/altruistic	Mostly altruistic	Completely altruistic

E. Your boss comes to you with a problem that he needs your help with. There is a big issue in another department, and he is requesting that you send your five top people to help fix the problem over the next two weeks. You both acknowledge that it will impact the timing of projects in your group and agree that related timelines can and will slip a bit, which is acceptable. You are asked, "Can I count on you and your team to help out?" Consider the motivation style that you would naturally employ to tackle this issue. Where do you tend to fall on the continuum? Circle your response.

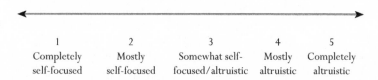

1	2	3	4	5
Completely self-focused	Mostly self-focused	Somewhat self-focused/altruistic	Mostly altruistic	Completely altruistic

Review the optimal response using the answer key.

A. You are at an off-site with your executive team to develop a vision for the go-forward division that you lead. The group has generally coalesced around a big vision that is slightly less ambitious than you had hoped. Despite your cajoling, the team is enthusiastically dug into their vision statement.

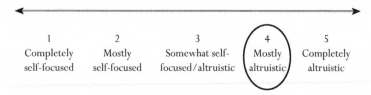

1	2	3	4	5
Completely self-focused	Mostly self-focused	Somewhat self-focused/altruistic	Mostly altruistic	Completely altruistic

It's an exciting and positive outcome if the group has joined hands around an ambitious vision for the future. Although it may be slightly less ambitious than the leader had envisioned, this is such a big win that the leader should proceed in a mostly altruistic fashion, embracing the team's approach to visioning.

B. Your company is facing a series of significant issues you are working through in some evening sessions with your executive team. On the home front, you have recently felt the need to spend more time with your twelve-year-old, who is struggling a bit in school. You've decided you can absolutely do both.

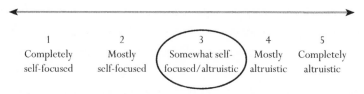

These are the difficult balance choices that most professionals have to make regularly. Perhaps it is obvious that these choices must be made with a balanced approach, acknowledging the organization's needs balanced against your personal life needs. The perfect balance is difficult to achieve, and these decisions normally require trade-offs. Most people believe (as I do) that you must first meet your key personal needs so that you can be a contributor at work, and therefore personal needs are the priority. However, the reality that, for example, the contract that has to be finalized today and your daughter's piano recital is this afternoon are real challenges for which we have to find a compromise. It takes a lot of balance.

C. The company is facing a big decision to sell a division. There is significant disagreement among the management team as to whether this is the right decision; some are strongly in favor, while some are strongly opposed. There are good arguments on both sides. You have never really believed in the potential of this business and are in favor of selling.

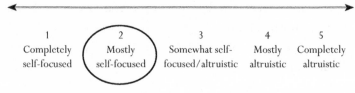

1	2	3	4	5
Completely self-focused	Mostly self-focused	Somewhat self-focused/altruistic	Mostly altruistic	Completely altruistic

Because this decision is big, it is perfectly acceptable for the leader to make the ultimate decision. In this case, several executives also support the sale of this division, which would allow the leader to approach this decision in a mostly self-driven (versus completely self-focused) fashion. The leader could acknowledge the rationale for keeping the business but lean a little harder into the reasons for selling and the support given by the executives who advocate selling. This would be an ideal opportunity for the leader to acknowledge the full leadership team's contributions to the evaluation and clearly articulate that the leader has made the final decision.

D. At your annual health checkup, your physician strongly advises that you dedicate some time to physical exercise. You tell her how demanding your job is and how you get in early and work late to be available to your teams when they need you. Your physician suggests blocking two early mornings each week as untouchable, during which you would start a modest exercise regimen. It seems possible, but you're not sure.

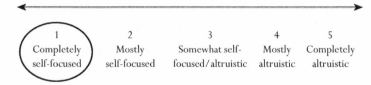

1	2	3	4	5
Completely self-focused	Mostly self-focused	Somewhat self-focused/altruistic	Mostly altruistic	Completely altruistic

Taking care of your physical health is an absolute priority, and it should always come before your professional obligations. This decision should be approached from a completely self-focused perspective.

E. Your boss comes to you with a problem that he needs your help with. There is a big issue in another department, and he is requesting that you send your five top people to help fix the problem over the next two weeks. You both acknowledge that it will impact the timing of projects in your group and agree that related timelines can and will slip a bit, which is acceptable. You are asked, "Can I count on you and your team to help out?"

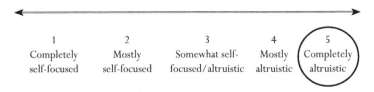

1	2	3	4	5
Completely self-focused	Mostly self-focused	Somewhat self-focused/altruistic	Mostly altruistic	Completely altruistic

This is one of those professional opportunities to do the right thing for the company, and the approach should be completely altruistic. Except in rare cases, the altruistic approach almost always serves the leader and their team well in the long run. Importantly, this leader clarified that this decision would impact the team's ability to reach their own goals in a timely fashion, which is an important component of enabling an entirely altruistic approach.

Summary: Note Your Tendencies

Look at your pattern of responses to the five scenarios across the seven facets of leadership. Do your responses tend to fall to the left side of the optimal response on the continuum of a particular facet?

Or are your responses falling to the right of the optimal responses? This is valuable information to increase your self-awareness and to strengthen your leadership skills.

To strengthen your skills, the next chapter presents some suggestions for each leadership facet.

CHAPTER 12

RECOMMENDATIONS

1. Communication

Direct communicator ◄——► Active listener

Consider when	*Consider when*
You are the obvious expert	Someone else is the expert
Diffusing a tense situation	Letting others sort things out
Framing a conversation	Engendering outcome ownership
Focusing a conversation	Observing and allowing others to lead

To be a more direct communicator:

- Dedicate time to developing and communicating a compelling vision. Simplify and make key messages real and relevant to different stakeholders. Describe this visionary future state in powerful terms. You can do this by answering the perennial employee question: "Why should I want to work hard to achieve the vision?"

- Ensure that every employee understands their role in making the vision a reality. To be intentional in key communications, consider these questions to crystallize the message you want to convey:
  - What are the key messages that need to be delivered?
  - What are the most effective ways to deliver these messages?
  - To whom should these messages be communicated? How often?
  - How will you know that communication has been effective?
- Convey important messages with powerful and emotionally appealing stories, not just rational explanations. Stories are memorable and can bring your vision to life. They also build trust when they feel genuine and personal. If this seems daunting, storytelling expert Annette Simmons (2007) suggests recalling times in your own life to help you get started. For example, consider times when you rose to the occasion or when you learned from failure.
- Recognize your preferred communication style as well as your audience's preferred ways of receiving information. Some employees need to be handled carefully, as they read into every sentence and gesture. Other individuals hear only direct and blunt communication. Tailor your message accordingly.
- For presentations to a group, practice and pay attention to your speaking style, tone of voice, and nonverbal messages. Asking for feedback from others on how you come across is an excellent step.

- Communicate, communicate, communicate. Repeat important messages frequently (e.g., your vision for the future, where the company is going, and the *why* behind the vision). People are busy and will likely not absorb your message the first time. When you think you've communicated enough, keep going.
- To ensure that employees clearly understand your message, ask them what they are taking away from the discussion. Concluding with specific follow-up actions and deliverable dates is a great way to ensure that both parties are crystal clear.
- Share what motivates you to engage and inspire people. Ask yourself, "What is exciting about the direction in which we're heading? What is the potential opportunity or upside in this situation?"
- Facilitate open dialogue to get your team's best thinking. Create a short list of go-to coaching questions (e.g., "Tell me the strongest argument in favor" or "Identify the strongest argument against"). As you communicate your perspective firmly, keep in mind that you are also a facilitator who works toward alignment.

To be a more active listener:

- Create a forum to listen to others. Hold regular one-on-one and team meetings to create space for open dialogue. Identify and frame issues that are ready for team input.
- Practice asking engaging open-ended questions and playing back what you hear from people. Have a few tried-and-true

questions in your back pocket, such as "Tell me more" or "I want to make sure I understand what you're saying. I heard you say…" Ask, "What is on your mind?" or "What do you want to do next?," and listen to the responses.

- Insert deliberate pauses for reflection into conversations. Note subtleties in what others are asking or saying. Use silence to give people time to think. Concentrate on understanding what is being said instead of formulating your response.

- Catch yourself before you interrupt or talk over someone. Resist the urge to give the answer when it could or should be someone else's place to do so. Pause even when you think you already know the answer or feel the urge to say, "Next!"

- If the team or an individual is planning to go in a direction different from one you would have selected, before you insert yourself to change the direction, ask yourself a few questions: Is it possible that another direction might be better? If the team or individual's recommendation is followed, what's the worst that could happen (if low cost, perhaps worth the risk?), and could there be an important learning by agreeing to the alternate path?

- Be fully present and give people your undivided attention. Try to avoid multitasking, such as checking your cell phone or looking at your computer screen for emails. Turn off your cell phone ringer, close the windows on your computer, put aside nonpertinent papers, and clear your desk. Pull out a notebook and take notes.

- One way to ensure that you are actively listening is to practice mirroring: repeating or summarizing what you are hearing from others. "If I understand correctly, Sandy, you and your team do not believe that you have the support for…" Mirroring provides the added benefit of reinforcing to others that you are truly listening.

- Note whether your tone of voice and body language convey to people that you are truly interested rather than disinterested, distracted, or busy. Respond in a way that communicates that you are listening: "That is really helpful information as I think about next year's budget. Could you tell me more about…?"

- Let people know about limits on your time and set clear parameters at the start. "I'm free to talk with you until noon." Until that time arrives, give your full attention to the person you are with and take the time to fully listen to what the person has to say.

- If you're busy or distracted when a colleague or direct report comes by your office, tell them that you want to give them your full attention and advise them on a better time to talk.

2. Rigidity

Principled ◄─────────────► Adaptive

Consider when

Relying on core beliefs to make decisions

Applying strong principles to your leadership approach

Staying true to your deeply held beliefs

Expecting the company to act consistently with your core beliefs

Taking a strong principled position on an issue

Acting consistently across similar types of uncertainties

Consider when

Being receptive to having core beliefs challenged

Acknowledging and respecting the different beliefs of others

Remaining open to listening to and learning from others

Taking a depends-on-the-facts-of-the-situation approach

Requesting data to correct or update your assumptions

Delegating decisions to those with more current or relevant experience

To be more principled:

- Identify which of your values and beliefs are nonnegotiable. Make them clear to your colleagues and employees. Point out when you make a decision based on these nonnegotiable principles.
- Where possible, communicate decisions with their principle basis. "The company will support the XYZ Foundation because we are an organization that values..." This reinforces those principles across the organization.

- Reid Hoffman (2018), founder of LinkedIn said, "Trust equals consistency plus time." Behave consistently in alignment with your principles and the core values of your company. Keep an eye open for situations in which you tend to waver based on others' opinions.

- Stay focused on key results in an objective way. You can do this by monitoring individual, team, and overall performance regularly. Holding yourself and your employees accountable for achieving measurable results reinforces a message of credibility and follow-through on commitments.

- Ensure clear expectations for each person's role and deliverables. Give employees flexibility to determine *how* they will execute plans and to question the status quo.

- Use structure to anticipate likely issues ahead of time. Start by becoming aware of early warning signs of crises in your business. Outline these early red flags, potential risks, and contingency plans to avoid problems or address unavoidable scenarios.

- Build deliberate pauses into your decision-making. Take the time to reflect before speaking on hot topics or when the stakes are high. Before making an important decision, step back, survey the situation, and remind yourself of your core principles. What do you really want in this situation?

To be more adaptive:

- Observe any tendency to overly attach to familiar ways of thinking and behaving. Get into the habit of asking yourself, "What's a better way to accomplish this?"

- Give yourself permission to pivot. Although follow-through is generally a good thing, don't stick to agreed-upon plans at any cost. Acknowledge mistakes or change positions if you have taken a wrong turn or new information indicates a need to adapt to change.

- Remember that a key word in leadership is *calibrate*. As situations change and evolve, don't continue to practice old behaviors in new settings. Increase your situational awareness and pilot new ways of working. Consider how past experiences and skills are applicable to new challenges and where you would benefit from tweaking your approach. As you consider eliminating practices that no longer fit a changing environment, distinguish the essential from the expendable. What is so precious and central to your organization's identity and capacity that it must be preserved? What, even if valued by many, must be left behind to move forward?

- As creatures of habit, looking at our world from a different lens is a valuable exercise. Jot down a few of your set routines, even if they're small. Then shake that routine up. For example, try a new restaurant and order an inventive dish, read a book from a different genre, or listen to a podcast about a different industry.

- Watch for new patterns. For example, you've never thought it was appropriate for employees to wear jeans to work, but you notice an increasing number of people and companies are moving to a more casual dress code (including jeans). It's time to revisit your position on jeans. Be observant. When you consistently start to see a new pattern, it is likely time to revisit a preconceived notion.

- Release your certainty in conversations regarding change. Adopt a growth mind-set by framing challenges as learning opportunities. What can you learn by asking questions and exploring new information with curiosity? This mind-set will release you from feeling that you need to have all the answers. You will gain new information and overlooked perspectives to confidently lead your team's response.
- Give others context when you change lanes. To help others understand your logic and decision-making, communicate the reasons for shifting from a particular course of action.

3. Goal Setting

Optimistic ◄————————► Realistic

Consider when	*Consider when*
Making dramatic course correction	Making financial commitments
Facing difficult short-term challenges	Rebuilding credibility
Balancing another's limiting practicality	Balancing another's overoptimism
Dreaming	Breaking down vision into tactics

To be more optimistic:

- Take a tip from professional athletes and visualize successful outcomes. Imagine things going well over a sustainable period of time and how this successful future would look. Use imagery to picture positive outcomes (e.g., picturing yourself successfully delivering the presentation to the executive team or becoming the number one company in your category). Mental images are powerful motivators for gaining extra energy and communicating a vision with enthusiasm.

- If you find yourself focused on an unsuccessful outcome, ask yourself, "Then what?" to understand what would actually happen in that scenario. Many times the answer is that nothing happens (e.g., an unsuccessful program has no impact on sales), and that realization is liberating. Even if you realize that there would be negative consequences of failure, assessing and understanding how bad *bad* actually would be is helpful. This approach allows you to ground yourself in reality instead of the worst-case scenario and to focus on actions toward successful outcomes.

- Encourage alternative approaches and new ideas. Work to improve new ideas rather than discourage them. When approached about a new idea, ask genuine questions to help incubate them. Resist the urge to automatically say no.

- Ask provocative, open-ended questions that encourage people to think differently (e.g., "How can we do this and that?"). Lead discussions and ask, "Could we do it if…?" as opposed to conversations that lean toward "We can't do it because…" Push to translate new ideas into actionable items and goals, not just talk.

- Energize people to go the extra mile with a positive goal and concrete ways to increase performance. Making objective feedback easy to obtain will help people track progress, which is very motivating. Celebrate milestones as well as personal and team bests. In fact, make it a point to find something (even if it's only a relatively small step forward) to celebrate and acknowledge progress.

- When reminding teams of the vision (which you'll need to do frequently), do so simply and succinctly and with enthusiasm (every time).

- Communicate stories of past wins and times when seemingly insurmountable obstacles were overcome. Use those stories to energize people during setbacks or challenges.

- Pay attention to how you explain events, such as the words you use (e.g., "we're choosing to..." versus "we have to..."). John F. Kennedy inspired a nation when he said, "We choose to go to the moon in this decade and do the other things, not because they are easy, but because they are hard..."

- Review your emails before hitting send. Are you unintentionally focusing on criticism with negative words? Emails heavily focused on the negative can disengage employees. You can deliver constructive feedback using positive words, which most people receive more openly and less defensively than negatively worded feedback.

- Watch your self-talk when you or your team are experiencing a setback. Notice and acknowledge your prevailing thoughts. Catch self-criticism or feelings of helplessness. Reality test the situation by asking, "Is that *really* true?" Try to coach yourself through setbacks with a more encouraging (and energizing) viewpoint.

- Practice seeing the opportunities in challenges. Write challenges down and then consider ways to reinterpret the situation:
  - Can anything good come from this situation?
  - What lessons can I learn?
- When communicating challenges to your team, keep the following things in mind:
  - Acknowledging the issue and putting it in perspective removes unnecessary tension and worry. People will relax a bit and focus on addressing the issue instead of stressing.
  - Remind yourself and others that a challenge is likely only temporary, not permanent.
  - Although the current challenge may affect a specific aspect of the business, it is not likely to ruin everything (e.g., our product recall may open the door for our competitors, but that doesn't mean we will lose all our customers and go out of business).
  - Be solution focused without blaming the problem on an individual or group; external factors likely affected the outcome as well. If you notice you or your colleagues getting stuck in a negative loop, stop rumination in its tracks and deliberately redirect attention elsewhere by thinking or doing something productive that could actually move you toward the goal. Consider putting concerns aside to allow negative emotion to subside and revisit at a later, specified time.
  - Concentrate on the things you and your team can control, and don't worry about those you cannot. Usually,

postmortems are most effective after the situation has been resolved, not in the heat of the moment.

o Setbacks are a normal and ordinary course of business. This may be another good rationale for why leaders must create an exciting long-term vision. If we are going on a meandering mountain hike and we stub our toe, perhaps we'll just turn back. If we are on a hike to reach a far-off summit, there is a completely different approach to the stubbed toe: deal with it, and then onward to the summit.

To be more realistic:

- Make sure that you're reading the circumstances accurately. Challenge your assumptions by looking for opposing evidence, searching for objective data, and testing your assumptions.

- Work to ensure that you don't shut down seemingly negative talk, which may be reality talk. Listen as objectively as possible, and process before reacting. Be aware that some people just need to know that the leader is aware of potential or existing problems before action planning.

- Shift your perspective. Step away and look at the current reality of the organization through the eyes of an outsider. What do you need to keep in mind? Consult with others, especially those with a different viewpoint. Seeing through others' lenses (and not just your own lens) will provide a broader view.

- When making important decisions, gather situational data from multiple sources and list the pros and cons of each choice.
- Acknowledge problems head-on and eat that frog (Tracy, 2017). If you put off thinking about potential risks or addressing challenges, they may become harder to address (and you'll become more reluctant to tackle them).
- When you find yourself feeling stuck, pick one thing and see it all the way through.
- Optimistic leaders must be careful not to allow their optimism to carry over into aggressive goal setting. Lofty goals that are consistently missed create a negative tone from which it is difficult to recover.
- Take a hard look at your preconceptions. Do you tend to view the world through rose-colored glasses, or do you tend to see problems in most cases? Ask someone to serve as a sounding board and help you think from a different angle (e.g., "You're focusing on the upside—let's talk about some of the possible risks").
  - Focus on clear, manageable team and individual goals. If you're not clear in communicating the goals, your people won't be clear either.
  - Establish sound outcome measures. Then find ways to pragmatically and objectively evaluate these measures on a regular basis.

4. Decision-Making

Directive ◄——————————► Delegative

Consider when	*Consider when*
You are the obvious expert	Someone else is the expert
Urgent action is required	There is time for discussion or reflection
There is critical impact	There is low business impact
There is no obvious learning opportunity	There is an obvious learning opportunity
It is not a key decision, and you have enough information	There is lack of clarity on an issue or solution
You are open to input, but none is offered	

To be more directive:

- When employees are not yet adequately skilled, deliberately give clear directions and expectations. A task that goes well beyond an individual's capabilities and stretch goals can lead to unnecessary anxiety and self-doubt. By providing expertise and needed structure, you are setting the person up for success. If you are unsure whether an employee is ready for completing a task on their own, ask yourself a question, such as "Is this person lacking the knowledge, experience, or confidence to complete the task?"

- Following up regularly on stated goals, expectations, and recommended approaches will limit disconnects and enable steady progress. Scheduling regular one-on-ones will allow you to check in, calibrate, and redirect, if necessary.

- When rules need to be strictly followed, such as in compliance issues, and you know these rules, be clear in explaining the rules, their importance, and the expectation for compliance.
- When an urgent decision is needed immediately or an emergency does not allow time to build consensus, confidently make a call and set the direction forward. This is not unlike taking charge to get people out the door when the building is on fire. Using this style only when needed will not negatively affect the climate of your team.
- When a leader with relevant expertise is tasked with kick-starting a turnaround, assessing the gaps and being directive about how to begin the rebuilding process can rally a possibly discouraged group and encourage future progress. Finding quick wins and celebrating early progress can build the group's confidence as it works toward proficiency.

To be more delegating:

- Determine the right time to allow others to lead. Decisions that don't require immediate action are excellent opportunities to engage others in discussion and tap into the expertise of your team. At these times, refrain from the pull to provide *the* answer. Instead, let individuals find their own answers. You might even want to count to ten in your head to give others room to speak up and lead. If your team is accustomed to you jumping in with the answer, expect some time for them to adjust. Don't be discouraged.

- When individuals on the team are confident and capable of reaching decisions about an issue, consider practicing a coaching approach. By asking powerful open-ended questions, you will help people focus on future possibilities, learn to make decisions, and hone judgment. This approach helps people become more self-sufficient, builds problem-solving skills, and removes you as a potential bottleneck to getting work done. Start by creating a list of questions that you can use in these coaching conversations (e.g., what do you want to accomplish? What options do you see? What are the next steps?).

- Coaching assumes that you will hone your active listening skills. Think about the last time you felt like someone was really listening to you. What did you appreciate about that interaction?

- Most people are not very good at listening to others. Even though they may appear to be listening, they are usually just waiting for their turn to speak. Get into the mind-set of listening to learn rather than listening to respond. Avoid planning your response while the other person is talking. Instead, aim to let them finish and then respond to what you actually heard.

- Pay close attention to what is (and is not) being said, including nonverbal communication (tone of voice, body language, gestures) and the spoken word.

- We think much faster than we talk, which means that we have to slow down our thinking when listening. Catch yourself when taking mental sidetracks and refocus on listening so that you are not missing the message.

- In ambiguous situations, use open-ended questions to push your team to search for additional information or expertise to make an excellent decision.

5. Intensity

Passionate ←—————————→ Patient

Consider when	*Consider when*
The problem or team requires intensity	A team or individual would benefit from space
There is fear or doubt among listeners	Problem resolution requires time
Lethargy needs to be countered	A group or individual is fragile
Urgency needs to be communicated	Things take time

To be more passionate:

- Remind people of the end game: By working hard, we can achieve the following…and imagine how that will feel. If we hit our stretch goal, we will get more resources for the future, earn a significant financial reward, be recognized by the company and our peers for excelling, and so on. Keep in mind what motivates the team and its members and describe the prize in those terms.

- Share your passion for your work with your team. When you spend time with your direct reports, tell them what you are excited to see in the business and why you find the work meaningful.

- Get specific on the timing of deliverables and milestones with input from the team. For instance, if the team can easily achieve the goal in two weeks, set a stretch goal of achieving the goal in a week. Engage the team by asking a question like this one: "Our goal is to get this done in two weeks. What would it take to get this done in one week?" Don't forget to recognize and reward the team when they hit the stretch goal.

- Increase how frequently you provide feedback to others. If you don't see the improvement you're looking for, emphasize the importance of the specific improvement(s).

- In addition to giving positive feedback to team members, recognize successful efforts and celebrate team achievements. When people are driving hard and working at a fast pace, they will burn out without pausing to recognize and enjoy success.

- When you become aware of a challenging situation or conversation, deal with it directly. When you start to realize that you are avoiding or postponing challenges, tell yourself to deal with it, and take prompt action.

- Practice being direct and candid in your communication. Clearly state what you want to say with both objectivity and empathy. Your team will appreciate not having to guess where you stand on key issues. Being straightforward and getting to the bottom line will save everyone's time.

- What drains your energy? Take an inventory of the things influencing your energy, such as typical sleep habits, exercise routine (or lack of), nutrition, demands on your schedule, and key relationships. As much as possible, limit your time with negative people who exhaust your energy reserves.

- Remember the law of diminishing returns. Keep your mental energy sharp by working in ninety-minute intervals. The brain uses up more glucose than any other bodily function. Typically, most glucose is spent after sixty to ninety minutes. Take a break (even a micro five-minute break) to recharge your energy. For instance, get up, go for a walk, have a snack, stretch, and so on.

To be more patient:

- Strengthen your problem-solving skill set. Start by clearly defining the problem as objectively as possible. Separate facts from assumptions, emotions, and reactions. Reframe the problem as a challenge that can be overcome. What are several options you could consider in an attempt to solve the problem? Don't automatically go with your first idea. Be planful by thinking through the pros and cons of each alternative. Decide on and implement your best possible solution (even if it's not ideal).

- Identify the things that test your patience and tend to trigger a high-energy or intense emotional response. Start by noticing changes such as physical sensations (increased heart rate, muscle tension, changes in your mood, intrusive thoughts, etc.). Once you become more mindful of your triggers, create strategies to put the brakes on strong emotions and force yourself to slow down. Some possible strategies include taking three deep breaths, counting backward from ten to one, visualizing a good outcome to the situation, or thinking of a relaxing vacation.

- Separate how quickly you would like something to change from how much time it will realistically take. For example, there could be a project with big potential results, but rushing it (e.g., inadequate planning or resourcing) would likely result in a poor outcome. Leaders need time to think these things through so that they approach them with appropriate intensity. Sending a team out at a sprinter's pace can be unwise if the project requires more of a marathon. In fact, directing a team to sprint when they know that they are embarking on a marathon is demotivating and not likely to achieve the desired team enthusiasm.

- When attempting to build patience, intention statements are a useful tool. Before you find yourself in a situation that you know will trigger an intense reaction, prepare go-to intention statements of how you'd prefer to handle those situations. One way is to ask yourself, "If my future self was looking back, how would I want to see myself handling the situation?" Then fill in these blanks: "When _____ happens, I will _____." An example intention statement looks like this: "When Sam's report contains multiple errors, I will take a deep breath, pause for five seconds, and calmly provide feedback on the needed revisions before our team meeting."

6. Compassion

Stern ←—————————→ Sensitive

Consider when	*Consider when*
The problem or team requires intensity	There is a personal or painful tragedy
There is fear among listeners	An employee needs to be heard
Lethargy needs to be countered	There is a fragile group or individual
There is a question about recoverability	Difficult failure needs to be acknowledged

To be sterner:

- Are there specific situations in which you find yourself tempted to keep your thoughts to yourself? Balance your concern for others with the business needs. Take some time to reflect and get clear on your own opinion and needs. Ask yourself, "What do I *really* think?" and "What is the ideal outcome I want to achieve?" Turn your responses to these questions into concise language you are willing to communicate. Practice as much as is necessary so that you can assert your needs and expectations confidently and directly.

- Losing a big client or experiencing a setback on a key project can be devastating for an engaged team. After acknowledging the loss and the natural reactions to it, help the team rally by brainstorming new approaches and taking action.

- Hold people accountable by communicating clear expectations and providing direct feedback on performance against those expectations. If an employee consistently underperforms (late on deliverables, repeated mistakes, etc.), state your observations objectively (i.e., share indisputable facts) and give them a chance, one-on-one, to discuss. Make this feedback session a two-way conversation. Share the effect of the behavior or action and ask, "Did you notice the client was upset?" or "Were you aware that you missed four key deliverables last month?" End with clear, specific future expectations, the time frame, and the potential consequences should the problem behavior not change: "Going forward, deliverables need to be on time or renegotiated if a timeline changes." A good motto when it comes to feedback is "no surprises." Schedule a follow-up check-in to ensure accountability.

- Mediocre performance from an individual or team is best countered with a resilient and uncompromising style. There are so many potential reasons why performance might be average, but successful leaders don't allow themselves to get distracted. Demanding improved or higher performance will get a group or individual focused on how to achieve those results. Note that these can easily slip back into excuses if leaders don't sustain focus on the desired outcomes.

- Express yourself in an assertive, positive, and respectful way. Pay attention to the message your body language is sending (posture, eye contact, tone of voice, etc.). You'll want your verbal and nonverbal communications to send the same message to other people. If your goal is to communicate a strong or uncompromising message, body language needs to be consistent.

- Use "I" statements to show that you are expressing your feelings and not those of the group. For example, "Going forward, I expect to see the following two items..." Avoid judgmental or exaggerated statements like "You never..." or "You always..." Rely on gathered facts and data.
- Know yourself and your values to identify your boundaries and stick to them. What are you willing to put up with? Articulate your needs and protect resources by saying no with confidence as necessary. Remember that frustration with other people often indicates that one of our boundaries has been crossed.

To be more sensitive:

- Being sensitive doesn't mean that you agree with what is being said. It does require allowing others to express their thoughts fully. Good listening skills are key. Listen carefully for the meaning behind what is being said. Reserve judgment and any urge to interrupt. Ask yourself, "How can I show that I am really listening?" At different points in the discussion, check in to make sure that you fully understand how the person is feeling. A good place to start is by asking simple open-ended questions to clarify, such as "Tell me more..." or "I want to make sure I understand what you're saying. I heard you say..."
- Pay attention to how others are reacting to a situation. Stay aware of the person's body language, facial expressions, and tone of voice. What can you learn through direct observation? Consider how your tone of voice and body language

express how you are feeling. Can you find a way to mirror the concern, frustration, rejection (or whatever they are signaling) to let them know that you understand where they are at this moment? Showing a person you understand is a big step in helping them feel supported.

- Take the time to get to know your people as individual human beings. For example, what does the employee value and care about? What are their interests? Who is important in their lives?

- Showing that you care for employees helps increase their loyalty. Act in a caring way, and look people in the eye. Show sincere interest and let them know that you care about what happens to them.

- Resist the temptation (if that is your natural tendency) to move the conversation too quickly to solution finding. In addition, the natural optimist leaders sometimes have to resist the temptation to find the good in situations. If the employee's house burns down, and you respond by saying, "At least no one was hurt," you may inadvertently be communicating that you don't understand the significance of the employee's issue. Sometimes the best response is simple acknowledgment.

- Remember that there is more to a difficult situation than the facts. By recognizing and acknowledging feelings and perceptions, people are more likely to feel heard and understood. When a person feels truly heard and understood, they move one step forward beyond the setback.

- Use "you" statements instead of "I" statements to express empathy. For instance, "It sounds like you're pretty worried about the deadline," or "It must seem to you that the team isn't taking this seriously enough."

- When you are frustrated by a colleague and know that you need to show more empathy in the moment, press pause. Suspend judgment for the moment and check your own emotions. By increasing awareness of what you're feeling and why you're feeling that way, you'll be more likely to strengthen your capacity to recognize others' perspectives and communicate with them adeptly.

- Share your own similar challenges in the past, but only after the other person has had a chance to share their perspective and feel heard.

7. Motivation

Self-focused ⬌ Altruistic

Consider when	*Consider when*
Achieving a big goal	The team has a big goal in mind
Questioning a key personal value	The value of the greater good is high
The downside of delegation is too high	The development or buy-in value of delegating is high
There is a high-risk decision and no right answer	
The leader's health or family is at risk	

To be more self-focused:

- Create a vision or master plan for your work and life. What do you really want for yourself? Clearly articulate your values and beliefs, and model them for others. Lead by example.
- Own your mistakes when you take a risk that does not pay off.
- Be self-directed and willing to stand your ground. Don't be swayed by popular opinion or second-guess a well-considered opinion. It is normal for people to disagree with you at times. Trust your own judgment and decisions without polling for other opinions or waiting for others to agree before making important decisions.
- Know yourself and increase your own self-awareness. Spend time alone, observe your personality in action, and clarify what motivates your behavior. Use these questions to jump-start your self-awareness:
  o If you were describing yourself, which three or four adjectives would you use?
  o What do you see as your greatest strengths? Keep those strengths in mind. They are likely areas where you should be more self-focused.
  o What is challenging about you? What is something about your personality that you wish you could change?
- Carve time out of your day for physical exercise at a time when you're least likely to cancel it. You will be more effective because of it.

- Remember, self-sacrifice can equal burnout. Set healthy boundaries to protect your time and energy so that you can show up at your best. Time away can provide recovery time for your focus and attention. Recognize when to step away from work so that you can return sharper. As a bonus, you will model productive behaviors for your direct reports.

To be more altruistic:

- Notice when you're thinking more about yourself than others in the organization. Ask yourself, "How do the goals set positively impact the team, the organization, and possibly the community?" Make decisions with the company and team in mind beyond self-interests.
- Look at issues through the lens of others. What are you missing? How will the decision affect them? Seek advice and ask for feedback.
- Offer opportunities for training and development by delegating decision-making and letting your direct reports stretch and grow. Make sure that they understand that you are still available if your assistance is needed. Offer both autonomy and support. Check in regularly to clarify expectations and offer feedback. Weigh the decision's importance; what's the worst that happens if they get it wrong? Many times, it is not too expensive. However, if the cost is high, or if you're just uncomfortable delegating, insert a review into the process to conduct a quality check to ensure that the team does not make the wrong decision.

- Share information and have an open-door policy to keep the lines of communication open with your team.
- Really think about whether you have buy-in on major initiatives. If you sense that you could use better or deeper buy-in, you may need to consider balancing your strong belief and perspective with a willingness to open up to broader input to have a plan with strong buy-in.
- Never ask anyone to do something that you would not be willing to do yourself. Roll up your sleeves and help when the team needs your expertise.
- Regularly ask yourself, "How can I use my leadership gifts to best serve others, my employees, my organization, or my community?"
- Coach individuals on your team. Use open-ended questions to help them identify their strengths and areas for development, and work with them to map out a plan to move toward their goals.

CHAPTER 13

CONCLUSION

We hope you have enjoyed *The Leadership Continuum* as much as we enjoyed writing it. Even though we've been practicing the art of leadership for many, many years, certain sections of this book reminded us of our own need to flex. Indeed, we all have natural tendencies—and that's perfectly all right. It's the inability or unwillingness to flex that gets us into trouble, limiting our leadership effectiveness and potentially slowing or stopping our leadership career trajectory.

Remember, the goal here is more effective leadership. A leader's goal is to help people and teams become emotionally engaged in working toward meaningful goals, move forward through various milestones toward achievement of those goals, and work through the inevitable obstacles along the way.

And you will make mistakes. We all do. Learn from those mistakes and keep moving forward. As you lead, commit to continuing your own development and allow yourself to get better and better. The ability to instinctively evaluate and move to that spot on the continuum that will maximize effectiveness gets better, faster, and easier with practice. Commit to your people's development and focus on identifying, developing, and creating your next generation of leaders. Developing young leaders is a worthwhile activity that regularly reminds experienced leaders how many different and equally effective leadership styles are out there.

Encourage those young leaders to make their own mistakes—and to learn from them. Urge those new leaders to develop their leadership skills by flexing across the leadership continuum, depending on the situation. Help them acquire the knowledge of when to flex right and when to flex left for maximum leadership impact. Perhaps one day an Emily, whom we met in the first chapter, will ask you about which leadership style is best, and you can simply slide a well-worn copy of this book across the desk.

Acknowledgments

We are grateful to many.

I want to thank the many talented people that I have had the opportunity to lead over the last thirty-plus years of my career. Leaders can only "lead" if people follow—and I want to thank all those who took a chance on/with me. While I am sure that I did not always succeed, I always endeavored to make better the organizations and people that I led.

I would also like to thank the many mentors that I have had over the years, from whom I learned so much. Many mentors were my bosses, but many others were colleagues, from whom I also learned so much. Some gave me direct feedback and counsel, but there were many other times where I learned by simply observing effective leadership in action. Thank you!

—Bill

Thank you to Bill Heiden for inviting us to collaborate.

Thank you to our partners, colleagues, and team members who read drafts, offered candid feedback, and supported our progress: Heather Getz, Sherry Bakhtian, Bob Kennedy, Noel Valenza, Julia Fabisiak.

We are grateful to our friends Rob Fazio and Margaret Smith for sharing their book-publishing perspectives with us.

To the leaders whom we have worked with and who have given us the privilege of working with their people, thank you. You are an inspiration to us, and we continue to learn from your example.

To those working to improve themselves and those around them, keep moving forward. You're not on this journey alone.

We both want to thank our parents, siblings, and children.

We want you all to thrive!

—Theresa and Cathleen

ABOUT THE AUTHORS

Bill Heiden is a highly experienced pharmaceutical/biotechnology executive, having served as a successful CEO in several public and private companies as well as serving as a director on several boards. Earlier in his career, he held a variety of senior leadership roles in the United States and internationally at Merck & Co. Mr. Heiden has an MBA from Cornell University's Johnson Graduate School of Management, a master's degree in international management from the University of Louvain (Belgium), and a BA in finance from the University of Florida. Mr. Heiden lives in the Boston area with his wife.

Theresa Hoffman is cofounder of Thrive Leadership, a firm whose workshops, executive coaching, and assessments help clients gain measurable results in leadership effectiveness, team alignment, and employee engagement. She specializes in emotional intelligence, motivation, and behavior change that leads to greater employee engagement. As an experienced executive coach, Theresa has worked with hundreds of leaders and their teams to build stronger self-awareness and relationship capital to have the greatest positive impact on others. Theresa lives outside of Philadelphia with her husband and three children.

Cathleen Swody, PhD, is cofounder of Thrive Leadership (www. thriveleadership.com). As an experienced industrial/organizational psychologist, Cathleen has analyzed thousands of 360 assessments and surveys and applies this expertise to help leaders reality check assumptions and better understand employees. Cathleen's insights have appeared in the *Wall Street Journal, Fortune, Fast Company*, and other media. She has served as an adjunct faculty member of the University of Connecticut School of Business. Cathleen lives in Connecticut with her husband and children.

REFERENCES

Bloom, P. (2016). *Against empathy: The case for rational compassion.* New York, NY: Ecco Press.

Cooper, R. K., & Sawaf, A. (1997). *Executive EQ: Emotional intelligence in leadership and organizations.* New York, NY: The Berkley Publishing Group.

Duckworth, A. (2016). *Grit: The power of passion and perseverance.* New York, NY: Scribner.

Gentry, W. A., Weber, T. J., & Sadri, G. (2016). *Empathy in the workplace: A tool for effective leadership.* Center for Creative Leadership. Retrieved from https://cclinnovation.org/wp-content/uploads/2020/03/empathyintheworkplace.pdf

Goleman, D. (2000). *Leadership that gets results.* Boston, MA: Harvard Business Review Press.

Henningsen, D. D., Henningsen, M. L. M., Jakobsen, L., & Borton, I. (2004). It's good to be leader: The influence of randomly and systematically selected leaders on decision-making groups. *Group Dynamics: Theory, Research, and Practice, 8*(1), 62–76.

Hoffman, R. (Host). (2018, September 18). *Masters of scale with Reid Hoffman* [Audio podcast]. Retrieved from https://mastersofscale.com/daniel-ek-how-to-build-trust-fast

Kouzes, J. M., & Posner, B. Z. (2011). *The leadership challenge.* San Francisco, CA: Jossey-Bass.

Rosete, D., & Ciarrochi, J. (2005). Emotional intelligence and its relationship to workplace performance outcomes of leadership effectiveness. *Leadership & Organization Development Journal, 26*(5), 388–399.

Seligman, M. E. P. (1990). *Learned optimism.* New York, NY: Knopf.

Simmons, A. (2007). *Whoever tells the best story wins: How to use your own stories to communicate with power and impact.* New York, NY: American Management Association.

Stein, S. J. (2017). *The EQ leader: Instilling passion, creating shared goals, and building meaningful organizations through emotional intelligence.* Hoboken, NJ: Wiley.

Tracy, B. (2017). *Eat that frog! 21 great ways to stop procrastinating and get more done in less time.* Oakland, CA: Berrett-Koehler.

Zaccaro, S. J. (2010). *The search for executive talent: Understanding the process and setting it in motion.* Alexandria, VA: SHRM Foundation.

Zenger, J., & Folkman, J. (2014, December 15). Research: 10 traits of innovative leaders. *Harvard Business Review.* Retrieved from https://hbr.org/2014/12/research-10-traits-of-innovative-leaders

Made in the USA
Monee, IL
16 January 2021

57815274R00090